HONEY
FROM THE ROCK

Jewish Lights Books by Lawrence Kushner

The Book of Letters: A Mystical Hebrew Alphabet

The Book of Words: Talking Spiritual Life, Living Spiritual Talk

Eyes Remade for Wonder: A Lawrence Kushner Reader

Filling Words with Light: Hasidic and Mystical Reflections on Jewish Prayer
with Nehemia Polen

God Was in This Place & I, i Did Not Know:
Finding Self, Spirituality and Ultimate Meaning

Honey from the Rock: An Introduction to Jewish Mysticism

Invisible Lines of Connection: Sacred Stories of the Ordinary

Jewish Spirituality: A Brief Introduction for Christians

The River of Light: Jewish Mystical Awareness

The Way Into Jewish Mystical Tradition

For Children

Because Nothing Looks Like God
with Karen Kushner

The Book of Miracles: A Young Person's Guide
to Jewish Spiritual Awareness

How Does God Make Things Happen?
with Karen Kushner
(SkyLight Paths Publishing)

In God's Hands
with Gary Schmidt

What Does God Look Like?
with Karen Kushner
(SkyLight Paths Publishing)

Where Is God?
with Karen Kushner
(SkyLight Paths Publishing)

בס"ד

HONEY
from the
ROCK

דְּבַשׁ מִסֶּלַע

D'vash MiSela

An Introduction to Jewish Mysticism
New Anniversary Edition

by
LAWRENCE KUSHNER

JEWISH LIGHTS Publishing
Woodstock, Vermont

Honey from the Rock (D'vash misela), Anniversary Edition

JEWISH LIGHTS Publishing Second Edition, Fourth printing, 2005
JEWISH LIGHTS Publishing Second Edition, Third printing, 2003
JEWISH LIGHTS Publishing Second Edition, Second printing, 2001
JEWISH LIGHTS Publishing Second Edition, First printing, 2000
JEWISH LIGHTS Publishing First Edition, 1990
Quality Paperback Book Club Edition, 1995
Harper & Row Publishers, Inc., New York, First Edition, 1977
© 2000 by Lawrence Kushner

For information regarding permission to reprint material from this book, please mail or fax your request in writing to Jewish Lights Publishing, Permissions Department, at the address / fax number listed below, or e-mail your request to permissions@jewishlights.com.

Library of Congress Cataloging-in-Publication Data
Kushner, Lawrence, 1943–
Honey from the rock : an introduction to Jewish mysticism / by Lawrence Kushner.—Jewish Lights Pub. anniversary ed.
    p. cm.
Previously published: Woodstock, Vt. : Jewish Lights Pub., 1990.
Includes bibliographical references.
ISBN 1-58023-073-3 (pbk.)
1. Mysticism—Judaism. 2. Jewish meditations. I. Title.
BM723 .K87 1999
296.7'12—dc21
                                                                    99-052238

10 9 8 7 6 5 4

Manufactured in the United States of America
Book design and illustration: Lawrence Kushner
Cover design: Lawrence Kushner and Bronwen Battaglia
Cover art: Lawrence Kushner

For People of All Faiths, All Backgrounds
Published by Jewish Lights Publishing
A Division of LongHill Partners, Inc.
Sunset Farm Offices, Route 4, P.O. Box 237
Woodstock, Vermont 05091
Tel: (802) 457-4000 Fax: (802) 457-4004
www.jewishlights.com

for
my parents

Aid and Miriam Kushner
the Heaven and the Earth

Ten Gateways to Jewish Mysticism

PUBLISHER'S PREFACE
to the Anniversary Edition
of *Honey from the Rock*

Life-changing events sometimes present themselves in disarmingly simple ways. Or, as Lawrence Kushner explains in this life-changing book, someone else may have some of the pieces you need to figure out the puzzle of your life. He writes:

Everyone carries with them at least one and probably
Many pieces to someone else's puzzle.
Sometimes they know it.
Sometimes they don't.

And when you present your piece
Which is worthless to you,
To another, whether you know it or not,
Whether they know it or not,
You are a messenger from the Most High.

It was 10 years ago that I attended a summer study retreat at which Lawrence Kushner was one of the teachers. An acquaintance walked over to me and said: "Did you know that three of Larry's books are out of print?" I didn't know that Larry had written a book, and wasn't sure why I should care. "Why are you telling me?" I asked. He thought I was "in publishing" because I had recently brought a book back into print. I explained that one book does not a publisher make, laughed and moved on.

But because I found Larry to be one of the most inspiring and interesting teachers I had experienced, I began to think about what might be done to bring his books back into print, to extend the reach of his inspiring voice. It was a time when the word "spirituality" did not trip so lightly off the tongue as it does now. After several months of thinking and talking to other teachers and spiritual seekers, my wife and I realized that there was a great need for someone to bring people words for the soul based on the Jewish wisdom tradition, words to help people find greater meaning in their lives—words like those found in *Honey from the Rock.*

Simply put, no publisher was focusing on meeting the needs of people like us. So, we started Jewish Lights Publishing to bring Larry Kushner's books back into print, to help people find the missing pieces of their puzzles. It was supposed to be just a small thing.

Dozens of people have told me that *Honey from the Rock* is a book that has affected their lives. Some have found new faith, some new understanding, others have repaired relationships. It has certainly affected *my* life. What grew out of that life-changing simple question, "Did you know that three of Larry's books are out of print?," is a publishing house that now is approaching the sale of its millionth book in English, with dozens of works translated into Portuguese, Polish, Korean, Italian and ten other languages. The response has been beyond anything we imagined when we began.

In the past decade I've read *Honey from the Rock* at least half a dozen times. Every time I read it I wonder if I have ever read it before. Either it keeps changing, or I do. Maybe it's both. There is a magical quality to it. Dip in at random and you'll see for yourself. As someone told me: "Larry is a mystic. He gives you flashes of insight."

Honey from the Rock, as do the many Jewish Lights books which have followed it, talks to people of *all* faiths, *all* backgrounds. We hope that your life will be touched by it, as our lives have been. Take a taste and find out. There may be a piece of your life's puzzle in here.

Stuart M. Matlins, Publisher

FOREWORD
to the Jewish Lights Edition
of *Honey from the Rock*

One of my teachers, Rabbi Eugene Borowitz, once quipped
that what we American Jews needed was a way to "make a
Motzi" (the traditional blessing over bread) at McDonald's. He
was speaking about the challenge of integrating ancient religious practice with contemporary a-religious culture.

In a sense, *Honey from the Rock* is an attempt to synthesize some
of the world view of classical Jewish mysticism, or Kabbalah,
with the ordinary life experience of its author. In retrospect,
even though some of the stories and Kabbalistic insights now
seem to me naive, nevertheless, taken all together, I believe
that the synthesis still holds. Indeed, the importance of the
book, now over a decade later, seems to be that an American,
born and raised Reform Jew would even try to understand his
moments of religious insight in the imagery of the Kabbalah,
or conversely, that such a writer would attempt to understand
the Kabbalah through ordinary 20th century life experiences.
And for this reason, *HONEY* works best, not as a primer on
Kabbalah, nor as a glimpse into the private places of a liberal
Rabbi, but as a means of enticing the reader to allow a Kabbal-

istic world view to inform his or her everyday life experiences. One can be, if not a Kabbalist, then at least their legitimate and reverent heir, even in this day. The ancient mysteries still instruct us.

One further observation is relevant. When *Honey from the Rock* was first written, the word "spiritual" was in its infancy in the Jewish lexicon. To be sure, the word had long been a staple in the Christian community even as Jews had sophisticated "spiritual" traditions under other names. But for reasons which we must leave to historians, as recently as a decade ago, Jews by and large did not use the word "spiritual" with any frequency or consistency. It is now commonplace, even hackneyed. I now believe that "spiritual" has become a code word for authentically or personally religious.

"Religious," alas, can mean too many things which are simply not religious. But "spiritual" seems to evoke the essence of whatever is personally religious. The original hardcover subtitle of *HONEY* was "Visions of Jewish Spiritual Renewal," but Harper & Row (the book's first publisher) for the paperback edition apparently chose marketing over theology and with it the subtitle, "Ten Gates to Jewish Mysticism." Somehow, as recently as ten years ago mystical sold more books than spiritual.

LSK
August 1990, Av 5750
Sandwich, MA

INTRODUCTION

הַקְדָמָה

א/1

There is a place that is as far from here as breathing out is from breathing in. *For the word is very near to you,* כִּי־קָרוֹב אֵלֶיךָ הַדָּבָר מְאֹד. Where life forever holds gentle sway over death, where people are human with the same grace that a willow is a willow, where the struggle and the yearning between male and female is at last resolved.

Deuter-onomy 30:14

It is to begin with, all inside us. But because we are all miniature versions of the universe, it is also found far beyond. And because we are all biologically and spiritually part of the first man, the place preceded us. And because we all carry within us the genotype and vision of the last man, the place is foretold in us.

There is no surprise in any of this. We have all known it all since before we were conceived by our most recent mother and father. So do not be confused if sometimes the place seems as real as your house or as illusory as your happiness. Only know in advance and instead that ordinary words will not be vessels or stores for some kinds of knowing.

ב/2

There is a legend that tells that the first Torah which the Holy One showed Moses, our teacher, was written *in black fire on white fire* עַל גַּבֵּי אֵשׁ לְבָנָה בְּאֵשׁ שְׁחוֹרָה. And that in each letter and each line and each crownlet of each letter are entrances to worlds of awareness.

Tanhuma
Bereshet
1

There is not a word or even so much as a letter of what the Holy One has given that does not contain precious mysteries. לֵית לָךְ מִלָּה בְּאוֹרַיְיתָא אוֹ אוֹת חַד בְּאוֹרַיְיתָא דְּלָא אִית בֵּיה רָזִין יַקִּירִין וְעִלָאִין

Zohar
III
174b

And that furthermore and at the same time there is a whole other Torah written in white letters in what we sometimes think are the spaces between the black letters. (Gershom Scholem, *On the Kabbalah and its Symbolism*, Schocken, 1965, p. 82)

Psychologists teach us that the mind is capable of perceiving either the relief or the background but we cannot perceive both at one time. We can literally see either two faces or a grecian urn at one time. We cannot see both simultaneously. Everything we know says that one thing cannot be two things at the same time. And yet we know that two things are one thing at one and the very same time.

Or here is a drawing of two *Alefs*. Not one but two.

But sometimes we refuse to believe our eyes. There is a kind of awareness that defies logic and is seduced by the mystery of paradox; it stubbornly returns time and time again to the utterly impossible task of bringing back with it convincing souvenirs of that place which is certainly our cradle and our goal. And probably eternal life if there be such a thing. Which is as far from here as breathing out is from breathing in.

ג/3

Near the end of Deuteronomy there is a long and ancient poem. Moses reminds the children of Jacob about their history and destiny: That though they wander the wilderness yet even there in that unlikely place they will find nourishment.

Deuter-
onomy
32:7,10,13

Remember the days of old . . .

זְכֹר יְמוֹת עוֹלָם . . .

He found him in the wilderness land . . .

. . . יִמְצָאֵהוּ בְּאֶרֶץ מִדְבָּר

He set him upon the high places of the earth

יַרְכִּבֵהוּ עַל־בָּמֳתֵי אָרֶץ

That he might eat the yield of the land

וַיֹּאכַל תְּנוּבֹת שָׂדָי

That he might suckle honey from the rock

וַיֵּנִקֵהוּ דְבַשׁ מִסֶּלַע

For us too the everyday world seems strewn with rocks. We fear that we have been led out into this wilderness to perish. That our yearning for holiness will be forever unfulfilled. And then at that moment, from something as mundane as a rock, there glistens a drop of that eternal baby food, honey. Even here there is spiritual nourishment. And so we eat a little and are satisfied and go on our way. Unable to tell others in words or remind ourselves about how the Holy One feeds us with honey from rocks. Nevertheless we try to remember. "Remember the days of old."

[14]

ד/4

There is a way of knowing that is only awareness. And because what was experienced was not experienced in words, it cannot be remembered or told or even reexperienced in words. There is a dim, awesome yearning sensation some people have at the back of their jaws which doctors suspect is a recollection of a suckling infant who obviously had but one way to recall a mother's breast. *A land flowing with milk and honey.* אֶרֶץ זָבַת חָלָב וּדְבָשׁ

Exodus 3:8

Sometimes even religions become ossified. The holy encounters that they carry seem hopelessly encrusted by centuries of mindless repetition. But we must nevertheless never forget that spiritual light cannot be extinguished. Only buried. And that for this reason every spiritual discovery is but a rediscovery. Nothing in this book is new. It has all been told before. This will be perhaps only another way to tell of the spiritual encounters that fill our lives.

ה/5

Every religious revival seems to be accompanied by a rebirth of the narrative as a vehicle for religious truth.

The stories tell you from where you have come. Your father was this and not that. And in doing so they foretell your destiny.

The great stories did not happen to the masters of old alone. They happen to us. You and I. This moment. A tale unfolds.

It is only that we have lost the narrative element of our existence. How could my life possibly be a spiritual tale? I must surely be a secular drone. But even that confession is the nucleus of a religious tale! If Moses, our teacher, had your definition of spiritual he would have remained an Egyptian too. Never entered the wilderness. For you see, we are the stories.

And for this reason there can be no honest telling about holy encounters without sharing them in their context. All true theology must finally be personal. God meets one of us. And we in turn are compelled to tell a story from which no objective theological truth can be distilled. For this reason authentic God-talk must always begin with the introduction *ma'aseh sh'hayah,* "It once happened . . ."

٦/6

Believing in God

Once I was to lead a Shabbos afternoon discussion with some grade school children from the congregation. I wanted to talk with them about holy matters and so I asked them if they believed in God. I thought that some would and some wouldn't and that we would have a lively discussion. But to my astonishment, no one raised a hand. They were not spiteful or disinterested or even impious. As a matter of fact, they were serious, interested, and honest. And by their silence they were simply saying that they did not believe in God. In much the same way that they might have said matter of factly that it wasn't raining.

My surprise soon became sadness. This must surely be the end of the line. The final despiritualization of American Jews. So we spoke about other things; I don't remember what. I only recall a great disappointment, a kind of finality and defeat. So it's come to this. Three thousand years of fire and piety for a bunch of spoiled rotten (I was mad) little suburban kids who unemotionally say they don't believe in God.

And then some time later on (during that same unremembered discussion), I thought of a different question. Or maybe it was the same question. I asked them if any of them had ever been close to God. And every one of them raised their hands. Freely and naturally. Unaware of any contradiction or inconsistency. But now I had to have proof, so I asked them when and where. And one by one they described, what I believe to be, the Jewish experience of God. One told of the previous evening when we had lit the Shabbos candles. Another of a few months ago amidst anger and sadness upon the death of a grandparent. And still another of a few days earlier when even though they didn't feel like it, they helped one of their parents.

‏א‎/7

The following pages are about "having been close." They are not so much about "knowing" as "being." Once it must have made sense to say that you believed in something, or had faith in something. But not any more.

Once we were obsessed with searching after holiness. Making its truth real in our lives. But after a while we turned instead to either compulsively repeating what our parents had discovered or mindlessly demystifying what they had piously handed down. Now we seek the great mystery in sensitivity groups, by psychic aberrations, or on drugs. Now it seems we are slaves to each new pseudo-spiritual secular fad, or birds faithfully laying traditional eggs that we have long ago quit expecting to hatch new life. Now nothing is left.

And this must surely mean it is time once again to set out for the wilderness.

I must make mention here of some of my fellow students and teachers: Everett Gendler, Nehemia Polen, Henry Zoob and especially Daniel Matt without whose great learning and patience much of our holy tradition would have remained beyond my reach. And the one who has sparked so much of the rekindling of American Jewish spirituality, Zalman. And my life-partner, Karen, whose love has made it possible for me to trust the meditations of my heart enough to share them here.

On this sixth day of the week, during which we read: *And Caleb stilled the people before Moses, and said, "Let us go up at once and make it ours for we are able to attain it."* וַיַּהַס כָּלֵב אֶת־הָעָם אֶל־מֹשֶׁה וַיֹּאמֶר עָלֹה נַעֲלֶה וְיָרַשְׁנוּ אֹתָהּ כִּי־יָכוֹל נוּכַל לָהּ.

Numbers 13:30

Five thousand seven hundred thirty-seven years
since the creation of the world.
Sudbury, Massachusetts

L.K.

1

הַמִּדְבָּר

HaMidbar

The Wilderness *of* Preparation

וַיַּסֵּב אֱלֹהִים אֶת־הָעָם דֶּרֶךְ הַמִּדְבָּר . . .

"God led the people around
by way of the wilderness . . ."

Exodus 13:18

ח/8

wilderness

The wilderness is not just a desert through which we wandered for forty years. It is a way of being. A place that demands being open to the flow of life around you. A place that demands being honest with yourself without regard to the cost in personal anxiety. A place that demands being present with all of yourself.

In the wilderness your possessions cannot surround you. Your preconceptions cannot protect you. Your logic cannot promise you the future. Your guilt can no longer place you safely in the past. You are left alone each day with an immediacy that astonishes, chastens, and exults. You see the world as if for the first time.

Now you might say that the promise of such spiritual awareness could only keep one with the greatest determination in the wilderness but for a moment or so. That such a way of being would be like breathing pure oxygen. We would live our lives in but a few hours and die of old age. *It is better for us to serve the Egyptians than to die in the wilderness.* כִּי טוֹב לָנוּ עֲבֹד אֶת־מִצְרַיִם מִמֻּתֵנוּ בַּמִּדְבָּר. And indeed, that is your choice.

Exodus 14:12

[22]

ט/9

It is no accident that we all began as slaves in Egypt. And that He, who is also known as a consuming fire, only once interceded in our affairs. To bring an entire people out into a wilderness where they could meet Him. He told them of a promised land but it was never delivered. Not to them. How long do you suppose it remained a secret? Ten years? Twenty years? Thirty years? No one could be that naive. Sooner or later everyone must have understood that this Ancient Only God did not really want them to get there; He only wanted them to be "on their way". (Which is the wilderness. What's your hurry? Where are you going? To the promised land? The other side of the wilderness? You aren't going to live the forty years. Your feet will never splash in the Jordan.)

For you and me life is not going to change.
From oasis to oasis, there will be enough food and water
    to live.
Modestly.
A tent.
Content.
A pillar of cloud by day.
A chevrolet.
A frame house with a white fence and a mortgage.
A screen door banging shut from children with
    sneakers and popsicles in summer.
A fire at night to keep the wild beasts away.

[23]

‏י‎/10

Abraham, our father,
Was simply told to leave.
Go forth from your land and from your kindred
  and even from your father's house.
To the land that I will show you.

Genesis
12:1 לֶךְ־לְךָ מֵאַרְצְךָ וּמִמּוֹלַדְתְּךָ וּמִבֵּית אָבִיךָ אֶל־הָאָרֶץ אֲשֶׁר אַרְאֶךָּ

This is the setting out.
The leaving of everything behind.
Leaving the social milieu. The preconceptions.
  The definitions. The language. The narrowed field
  of vision. The expectations.
No longer expecting relationships, memories, words, or
  letters to mean what they used to mean. To be, in a
  word: Open.

If you think you know what you will find,
Then you will find nothing.
If you expect nothing,
Then you will always be surprised.
And able to bless the One who creates the world anew
  each morning.
So it is with setting out on the path of liberation, leaving
  everything.

THE WILDERNESS OF PREPARATION

He would even have to discover
The way he would discover
While he was on the way.
Of him it was said, *A man who set out and did not know*
for which place he was destined.

יֵשׁ אָדָם שֶׁהוֹלֵךְ וְאֵינוֹ יוֹדֵעַ לְאֵיזֶה מָקוֹם הוּא הוֹלֵךְ

Tanhuma
Lekh-
Lekha
3

And then in the next generation Isaac had to set out with
his father
Take your son, your only son

קַח־נָא אֶת־בִּנְךָ אֶת־יְחִידְךָ

Genesis
22:2

As Abraham had to leave his father, Isaac must leave his
mother.

And then in the next generation, Jacob had to set out,
Leaving behind his father and his mother and his brother
And Jacob went out from Beer Sheba . . .

וַיֵּצֵא יַעֲקֹב מִבְּאֵר שָׁבַע

Genesis
28:10

And then in the next generation, Joseph had to set out,
Leaving behind brothers, mother, and father.
And they brought Joseph down to Egypt . . .

וַיָּבִיאוּ אֶת־יוֹסֵף מִצְרָיְמָה

Genesis
37:28

And then in the next generation of which there is record
Moses had to set out. *And Moses fled . . .*

וַיִּבְרַח מֹשֶׁה

Exodus
2:15

Leaving behind his people.
Again, another one alone in the wilderness.

Until at last all the people whose fathers had each
Set out in their generation.
Alone for the wilderness,
Leaving everything behind
Were at long last themselves ready
To leave the slave pits.
There are great oral traditions about how they had to be
tricked and manipulated into setting out. For to be sure,
no one who sets out ever does so eagerly.

But the children of Israel set out from Ramses . . .

Exodus וַיִּסְעוּ בְנֵי־יִשְׂרָאֵל מֵרַעְמְסֵס
12:37
Leaving everything behind them.
For a promised land.
But more probably,
Death in the wilderness.

Then there is being alone.
In the most God forsaken place.
Where God visits after all.
Leaving one's house and one's parents and one's family,
And finally the slave pits themselves
For a wilderness of no expectations.
Somewhere where I will learn what I will learn.
Where I can "see" what I will be.

Exodus אֶהְיֶה אֲשֶׁר אֶהְיֶה
3:14

One after another each of our fathers before us
With their strange Hebrew yen for the open places
Heard this ancient God's voice
Telling them to leave their preconceptions
For the wilderness.

יא/11

But He did not tell them to leave everything behind for we read that *Moses took the bones of Joseph with him.*

וַיִּקַּח מֹשֶׁה אֶת־עַצְמוֹת יוֹסֵף עִמּוֹ

Exodus 13:19

Scripture makes known the excellence of Moses: While all Israel were busy taking up Egypt's booty, Moses busied himself with taking up the bones of Joseph ...

לְהוֹדִיעַ שִׁבְחוֹ שֶׁל מֹשֶׁה, שֶׁכָּל יִשְׂרָאֵל עֲסוּקִין בְּבִיזָה, וּמֹשֶׁה עָסוּק בְּעַצְמוֹת יוֹסֵף ...

Pesikta deRab Kahana (Beshallah 10)

Rabbi Meir suggests that the people of each and every tribe were to take the bones of their own tribal father up with them.

ר' מֵאִיר אוֹמֵר ... שֶׁהֶעֱלָה כָּל שֵׁבֶט וְשֵׁבֶט עַצְמוֹת רֹאשׁ שִׁבְטוֹ עִמּוֹ

Ibid. (Beshallah 10,end)

Here is the scene. Everyone. is getting ready to leave. They bump into one another in their excitement. The car is loaded. The children are screaming. Now one last time. Did you forget anything? Oh my God! I forgot Joseph's bones. I don't even know where they're buried!

People say that it was Serah, daughter of Asher, who was still alive in that generation and told Moses "Moses, Joseph is buried in the Nile River ...".

אָמְרוּ שֶׂרַח בַּת אָשֵׁר הָיְתָה בְּאוֹתָהּ הַדּוֹר, אָמְרָה לְמֹשֶׁה בַּנִּלוֹס הַנָּהָר יוֹסֵף קָבוּר ...

Ibid. (Beshallah 10)

[27]

How will you ever get them now? Look. It's almost morning. We only have a few hours. "No." says Moses. "I must get the bones." (And this resolve is accorded one of his greatest deeds).

"I too once floated in a tiny ark on that river. I know it well." For while we must leave our preconceptions behind, we cannot set out for the wilderness without bringing with us those who have come before. Maybe that is why Joseph made us promise.

יִב/12

The Bar Mitzvah Guest

Sometimes I do a Bar Mitzvah once a week for many months in a row. And after the ceremony there is a great welling up of completion and pride and promise. Strangers who have come as invited guests come up to share their joy. And I try to listen to each one of them and respond, but it is very difficult. They all say pretty much the same thing — what else is there to say? And then last Shabbos there began one of those well intended but empty exchanges that sometimes populate the minutes of rabbis after a service. I said to a man, "Where are you from?" He said, "I don't know." (Just what I needed, an existentialist.) "C'mon, where are you from?" But again he insisted that he did not know. I looked more closely and saw that he was not an amnesia victim, a junkie, or an alcoholic. He was simply a human being who was moved by our worship experience and who had come forward. "Where are *you* from, Rabbi?" And then I realized what was going on and what I had learned. I told him that I didn't know where I was from either. For I understood then that I didn't. "In that case you understand what I'm trying to say," he said. And I did. And we parted.

י״ג/13

The wilderness is not just a desert through which we wandered for forty years. It is a way of being. Even if just for a moment every now and then each day. For it is the only way to begin.

One who does not make himself ownerless-open like the wilderness, will be unable to acquire human wisdom or God's word. That is why what was said was said in the wilderness, Sinai.

כָּל מִי שֶׁאֵינוֹ עוֹשֶׂה עַצְמוֹ כַּמִּדְבָּר הֶפְקֵר אֵינוֹ יָכוֹל לִקְנוֹת אֶת הַחָכְמָה וְהַתּוֹרָה לְכָךְ נֶאֱמַר בְּמִדְבַּר סִינַי

Numbers Rabba 1:7

And that must surely be why He brought us out there. For there and only there might we be able to encounter the mystery.

THE SECOND GATE

2

הַסוֹד

HaSod

The Mystery

בַּתְּחִילָה עָלָה בְּמַחֲשָׁבָה לִבְרֹאת ב׳
וּלְבַסּוֹף נִבְרָא אֶלָא אַחַת

"At first the intention was to create two
but ultimately only one was created"

Berachot 61a

mystery

יד/14

The first mystery is simply that there is a mystery.
A mystery that can never be explained or understood.
Only encountered from time to time.
Nothing is obvious. Everything conceals something else.
The Hebrew word for universe *Olam*
Comes from the word for hidden.
Something of the Holy One is hidden within.

טו/15

There is more to reality than meets the eye.
The everyday world is an illusion.
It is real only in the way a dream is real.
We see it and we hear it and indeed we live in it.
We stake our lives on it.
And in an instant it is gone.

טז/16

You are watching television. Then you turn the sound
way down like you used to do when you were a kid during the commercials and laugh at the funny lady whose

lips moved without making any sounds. Then you turn the contrast knob so that the speaker seems barely visible through some dark foggy mist. Then you turn the brightness all the way down so that the screen is completely black. You see nothing. You hear nothing. But you continue staring at the black soundless glass rectangle. For something is there. Someone is speaking and looking. Only you can't see them. From within a darkened space a message issues.

A reality that will not be seen or heard or understood. Just as the eye will never see itself.
But nevertheless there is something going on there.

י/17

The Baal Shem tells of a king who was a master at creating illusions. *The glory of God is to conceal a thing.*

כְּבֹד אֱלֹהִים הַסְתֵּר דָּבָר

Proverbs 25:2

And while he wanted very much to be close to his people, he wanted even more for his people to want to be close to him. So he devised a plan. He built around himself a great castle-illusion. There were illusory walls and doorways and towers. There were chambers and courtyards and passageways. And in front of each one the king placed illusory treasures of every kind. Bags of money, trips to Florida, and having a beautiful body. Then he proclaimed throughout the land that he wished to be found. And all the people came to the illusory castle

[33]

but one by one they gave up searching for the king and they settled instead for some illusory treasure. Until, at last, the king's son came. He saw that it was all an illusion and that his father was there in plain view, sitting on a folding chair in the middle of a great, open field.

*Keter
Shaym
Tov
Jerusalem
1968
p.13.*

וְעָשָׂה בַּאֲחִיזַת עֵינַיִם חוֹמוֹת וּמִגְדָּלִים וּשְׁעָרִים וְצִוָּה שֶׁיֵּלְכוּ ... אֶצְלוֹ דֶּרֶךְ הַשְּׁעָרִים וְהַמִּגְדָּלִים וְצִוָּה לְפַזֵּר בְּכָל שַׁעַר וְשַׁעַר אוֹצְרוֹת הַמֶּלֶךְ ... עַד שֶׁבְּנוֹ יְדִידוֹ הִתְאַמֵּץ מְאֹד שֶׁיֵּלֵךְ דַּוְקָא אֶל אָבִיו הַמֶּלֶךְ אָז רָאָה שֶׁאֵין שׁוּם מְחִיצָה מַפְסִיק בֵּינוֹ לְבֵין אָבִיו כִּי הַכֹּל הָיָה אֲחִיזַת עֵינַיִם ...

The great question, you see, is whether or not this world is really real. If it is, then those who would search for some higher reality are mistaken. If this world is illusory — but a screen for some higher order of being — then there is more to reality than meets the eye. And we have settled for some illusory treasure and given up searching for the king.

Religion is a more or less organized way of remembering that every mystery points to a higher reality. A reality overarching and infusing this world with splendor. One pulsing through its veins. Unnoticed and unnamed. Of the Nameless One. A holiness so holy that it fills even our every day illusions with spiritual meaning.

יח/18

Spiritual awareness is born of encounters with the mystery. It begins with an almost trivial passing

astonishment at the irreducable paradox that underlies everything. At the root of our perception of the world is a duality. There are two sides that are irreconcilable and mutually exclusive. But there they are, at the same time. Their simultaneous existence defies any known system of logic.

Once we had to leave our little ones with their grandparents for several weeks. We were leaving the next morning for Israel and they were boarding a plane with their grandmother for Detroit. I said to my little children — one of the few wise things I have ever said — that they, like their parents, were probably excited and happy and, at the same time, frightened and sad. And that was all right. That that was the way of the world. And so together we laughed and cried.

Just this is the mystery. That all the important moments, and probably at the source of all moments there is something that is illogical, paradoxical, and sort of impossible. Male and Female. Good and Bad. Loved and Hated. Sought and Shunned. Alive and Dead. *A time for loving and a time for hating.* עֵת לֶאֱהֹב וְעֵת לִשְׂנֹא *Ecclesiastes 3:8* Unfortunately, it is usually the same time.

When we said goodbye at the airport — the parents and the children — happiness and sadness were both there. And probably some simultaneous "Don't leave me" and "good riddance." But because the logic of this world demands that whenever experience offers two sides, only one of them can be good . . . the other must be named "bad" and removed from awareness.

But every now and then the paradox sparkles from within, and we are mystified and a little frightened and we pause. To live is to arbitrarily choose one but ever be bothered by the other. There is an epilogue to this story. Recently I reminded Noa and Zack about how "everything had some of its opposite within it." About how nothing can be all good. Zachary suggested that maple syrup is all good. But Noa said that even maple syrup gives you cavities.

God says, *I set before you this day the blessing and the* *Deuter-* *curse, . . . Choose life that you may live . . .*
onomy
30:19 נָתַ֤תִּי לְפָנֶ֨יךָ֙ הַבְּרָכָ֣ה וְהַקְּלָלָ֔ה וּבָחַרְתָּ֙ בַּחַיִּ֔ים לְמַ֖עַן תִּחְיֶֽה
But to choose the Nameless One is to choose both for only in His unity are both encompassed and resolved. For He is the mystery. The unexplainable One.

יט/19

God faces a similar dilemma. He must restrain His eagerness to reveal Himself to us without, on the other hand, sounding unimportant.

We read in the Midrash that:
Rabbi Juda bar Nehemyia explained that since Moses was a beginner when it came to hearing God's word, the Holy One reasoned: If I reveal myself to him in My awesome full voice, I run the risk of destroying him. On

*the other hand, if I speak with a soft voice, he will regard
My word as trivial.*

... אָמַר הַקָּדוֹשׁ בָּרוּךְ הוּא אִם נִגְלֶה אֲנִי עָלָיו בְּקוֹל גָּבֹהַּ אֲנִי
מְבַעֲתוֹ וְאִם בְּקוֹל נָמוּךְ בּוֹסֵר הוּא עַל הַנְּבוּאָה ...

*Exodus
Rabba
45:5*

The resolution of the paradox is the same as its source.
God becomes parent.
*What did the Holy One do? He revealed himself in the
voice of Moses' father. Cried Moses, "Father! You have
come out of Egypt!?" "No," he answered. "I am not
your father. Only the God of your father."*

... נִגְלֶה עָלָיו בְּקוֹלוֹ שֶׁל אָבִיו ...

*Ibid.
45:6*

And man becomes child. Afraid to confront the paradox,
man forsakes ultimate wisdom.
*Whereupon Moses hid his face. Rabbi Yehoshua bar
Karcha lamented, it is too bad that Moses hid his face. If
he hadn't hidden his face the Holy One would have
revealed to him what was above and what was below.
What was. And what would in the future come to be.*

... שֶׁאִלּוּלֵי שֶׁהִסְתִּיר פָּנָיו הָיָה מְגַלֶּה לוֹ הַקָּדוֹשׁ בָּרוּךְ הוּא מַה
לְמַעְלָן וּמַה לְמַטָּן ...

*Ibid.
45:5*

And now that we would return to the resolution once of-
fered everything has reverted to its opposite once again.
*But now, later on, when Moses wanted to see God, he
said, "Show me all your glory." The Holy One said,
"When I wanted to see you, you hid your face. And now
that you want to see Me, I don't want to see you. Man
shall not see Me and live."*

Exodus
Rabba
45:5

כְּשֶׁבִּקַּשְׁתִּי לֹא בִקַּשְׁתָּ עַכְשָׁו שֶׁבִּקַּשְׁתָּ אֵינִי מְבַקֵּשׁ. ...

Look at it this way: God who is the source of life cannot
be seen without certain death.

ב/20

Let us examine the paradox.
At the source of every great mystery are the twins, Jacob
   and Esau.
Jacob, a quiet man, dwelling in tents
One destined to become the progenitor of Israel
Who was at first filled with cunning and greed.
And Esau, his twin, a skillful hunter, a man
   of the field.
One destined to father the cruel tyranny of the Roman
   Empire.
Who was at first guilty only of being hungry.
Two who came from the same Mother.
How could it be that these two
Who were for one another day and night
Could have come from the same womb?
And just this is the mystery.
That beneath and before everything is its opposite.
An irreducible paradox.

THE MYSTERY

Eve bore both Cain and Abel.
Abraham fathered both Isaac and Ishmael.
And Rebecca bore both Jacob and Esau.
Two nations are in your womb.

שְׁנֵי גוֹיִם בְּבִטְנֵךְ

Genesis
25:23

*Rabbi Phineas and Rabbi Hilkiah said in the name of
Rabbi Simon that not even the thinness of a membrane
separated Esau and Jacob, yet the one came out a
righteous man and the other a wicked man.*

ר׳ פִּנְחָס ור׳ חִלְקִיָּה בְּשֵׁם ר׳ סִימַאי אֲפִילוּ דוֹפָן לֹא הָיָה בֵּינֵיהֶן
וְיָצָא זֶה צַדִּיק וְיָצָא זֶה רָשָׁע

*Pesikta
de Rab
Kahanah
(Shmini
Atzeret
30)*

That both father and mother are within each parent.
That hatred conceals love and love conceals hatred.
That life becomes death while death returns to life.
That sometimes evil is disguised as good while good
    is not as easy to understand as we once thought.
A piece of paper must, after all, have two sides.
*The voice is the voice of Jacob; and the hands are the
    hands of Esau!*

הַקֹּל קוֹל יַעֲקֹב וְהַיָּדַיִם יְדֵי עֵשָׂו

*Genesis
27:22*

And so it is, that encounters with the mystery
    do not bring mystery.
Instead, they bring religion into the world.
For this world cannot withstand the mystery.
And those who would bring the mystery to our
    awareness either
Destroy the world or create religion.

[39]

Religion takes the One who speaks to us from out of the
mystery,
*And there was a bush all aflame, yet the bush was not
consumed.*

*Exodus
3:2*

וְהִנֵּה הַסְּנֶה בֹּעֵר בָּאֵשׁ וְהַסְּנֶה אֵינֶנּוּ אֻכָּל

Religion takes the One who encompasses both light and
darkness,
*Praised are You O Lord . . . who forms light and creates
darkness.*

*Daily
Prayer-
book*

בָּרוּךְ אַתָּה יְיָ . . . יוֹצֵר אוֹר וּבוֹרֵא חֹשֶׁךְ

Religion takes the One who formed both man and
woman,
Male and Female He created them.

*Genesis
1:27*

זָכָר וּנְקֵבָה בָּרָא אֹתָם

Religion takes the One who makes both life and death,
The Lord gives and the Lord takes away.

*Job
1:21*

יְהוָה נָתַן וַיהוָה לָקָח

Religion takes experience of ultimate mystery,
The encounter with the Heaven and the Earth,
The Father of mysteries and Mother of paradox,
And teaches us to choose only blessing and life.

*Why did the Holy One create both the hell of Gehenna
and the heaven of the Garden of Eden? In order that one
may borrow room from the other. And how much space*

is there separating them? ... *The rabbis said that they
are right next to one another.*

מִפְּנֵי מָה בָּרָא הקב"ה גֵּהִינָם וְגַן עֵדֶן כְּדֵי שֶׁיִּהְיוּ מַצִילוֹת זוֹ מִזּוֹ
וְכַמָּה רֶיוַח יֵשׁ בֵּינֵיהֶם ... רַבָּנָן אַמְרֵי שְׁתֵּיהֶן שָׁווֹת

*Not even the thinness of a membrane separated Easu and
Jacob.*

אֲפִילוּ דוֹפָן לֹא הָיָה בֵּינֵיהֶן

*Pesikta
deRab
Kahanah
(Shmini
Atzeret
30)
Ibid*

The goal is the resolution of both.
The only way is through choosing one.
What was born of mystery returns to mystery.
That the only way to choose both
Is by choosing one.
In this way and no other can the unification be achieved.
In Rebecca's belly they still struggle,
Jacob and Esau,
But once they enter this world only one can be first.

Surely through His eyes, as it were,
We could see and even withstand
The Light in the Darkness
The Life in the Death
And the Good in the Bad.
But through our own eyes
We can only see one at a time.
A piece of paper can have only one side at a time.
But it must also have two sides at the same time.

*Tablets written on both sides; on one side and on the
other were they written.*

לֻחֹת כְּתֻבִים מִשְּׁנֵי עֶבְרֵיהֶם מִזֶּה וּמִזֶּה הֵם כְּתֻבִים

*Exodus
32:15*

Thus it is throughout the Torah, which contains two sides — revealed and hidden. And these two aspects are found everywhere both in this world and in the upper world.

Zohar II 230b

דְּכָל אָרְחֵי דְאוֹרַיְיתָא הָכִי הוּא אִתְגַּלְיָא וּסְתִימָא וְכָל מִלִין דְּעַלְמָא בֵּין דְּעַלְמָא דֵין וּבֵין דְּעַלְמָא דִּלְעֵילָא כֻּלְהוּ אִיהוּ טָמִיר וְגַלְיָא

כא/21

Genesis 1:27

Rabbi Shmuel commented on the verse, "Male and Female He created them" by suggesting that each was created with both. Two dimensions. *Two faces.*

Midrash Tehillim 139:5

דּוּ פַרְצוּפִין בְּרָאוֹ

Indeed there are two ways of knowing. Neither can understand the other and yet both need each other to survive.

It goes back to when you first learned that it took a woman and a man to create a new life. And that that preposterously simple union also intimated the Holy One. We read in *Pesikta Rabbati* it takes three to make a child — a man, a woman, and the Holy One blessed be He. מִפְּנֵי שֶׁשְׁלָשְׁתָּן שׁוּתָּפִים בּוֹ

Pesikta Rabbati 23/24

Now these two dimensions are more than bisexuality. They are present in the protoplasm of each cell in both men and women. They find correspondence in world cultures and in the halves of the brain (cf. David Bakan, *The Duality of Human Existence*, Beacon Press, 1966).

THE MYSTERY

The list of opposites is endless and ancient:

Light	Darkness
Heaven	Earth
Male	Female
Insight	Intuition
Perfection	Completeness
Strengthening	Nurturing
Left side of brain	Right side of brain
Right side of body	Left side of body
Rational	Mystical
Linear logic	Paradox
Verbal	Nonverbal
Western culture	Eastern culture
Individual	Communal
Doing	Being

The Jewish response to the holy comes historically from the juncture of East and West. It is a system eternally bent on synthesizing the two. For only by doing/being both at once can the religious endeavor maintain its intergrity.

Religion mediates between the two.

If spiritual awareness is being, then what do you do once you have reached such holiness? If living in this world is doing, then how shall you be while you are doing? You must sanctify the deed with the spirit and embody the spirit with the deed.

כב/22

*On watching your children at their school
when you are the honored guest*

Another way of understanding the paradox is to pretend that parents are God and their children are people like us. Here the wanting to be close is the reason for distance.

I remember so well when my father would visit class how I would shine with pride. That one is *my* Father. And I remember how I would practice great *Tzimtzum*, self-withdrawl, myself. (I must not let anyone know of our great love.) And all the while my Daddy is using great self-restraint himself in order to let his little one make the first move. Now it is my turn. Now I am the Daddy. I will just stand here and smile. You tell me how to act.

Last night I told him at bedtime, "Now don't tell anyone, but tomorrow your teacher has asked me to come and tell your class — the world — what I know about the Torah. Just wait till I show up. It will be our special secret." And the little boy is so excited he can't sleep.

And then when I show up he is fighting with some kid over a block. He doesn't see me. He is so precious to me. I feel tears of loving in my eyes. And then he sees me. He races to me. Jumps. Throws his arms around me. I

hold him in the air. So glad he can tell our secret. So glad he will make our love public. Now.

And then. All throughout the morning. Every now and then. He comes over. Wants to be picked up. Hugged again. I love it. Why conceal it. I'm his Daddy. We love one another.

There is much talk about God and His children. But we rarely get to be God and let our little sons and daughters show their love. Maybe everyone would love to be able to throw their arms around their daddy in front of their class but because of some terrible peer pressure, they are afraid. So they just sit there hoping their father doesn't make some error that will embarrass them. And then the father leaves, and the moment of hug-loving in public is lost forever.

We read that Dov Baer, the Magid of Mezritch, taught that *the Holy One, as it were, had to contract His brightness, like a father — who contracts his wisdom and speaks in childtalk for the sake of his little child. And indeed, so it is, that in such a way all childlikenesses* (wonder ? spontaneity ? immediacy ? playfulness ?) *are* (re-) *born in a father . . . And so it turns out that love causes withdrawal.*

צִמְצֵם הַשֵּׁ"י כִּבְיָכוֹל אֶת בְּהִירוּתוֹ כְּדִמְיוֹן אָב הַמְצַמְצֵם אֶת שִׂכְלוֹ וּמְדַבֵּר דִּבְרֵי קַטְנוּת בִּשְׁבִיל בְּנוֹ הַקָּטָן. וְגַם כָּל מִדּוֹת מַעֲשֶׂה נַעֲרוּת נוֹלָדִים בְּהָאָב . . . וְגַם הָאַהֲבָה גָּרְמָה אֶת הַצִּמְצוּם.

Magid
Devarav
LeYakov
1

[45]

כג /23

A Tree in Blossom

Fragance is the most mysterious of them all. So very subtle. Sensual. Unavoidable. Fleeting. You cannot help breathing. Encountering aroma.

The path I take to the synagogue winds through a small park in the center of town. And in the middle of the park is a tree that blooms with thousands of white clustered blossoms. The branches droop with the weight of their flowers. And if you walk under the tree, you must bend down and wend this way and that to avoid the foliage. The tree and the blossoms are everywhere. You only see a few inches ahead of you. As if on wheels you glide through the lush spring. And then you are out of it and it is gone.

But more than anything it is the fragrance that envelops you. For maybe a minute or so there is only the sensation of smell. You cannot see or feel or taste or touch. If only you could bask in this air forever. Join the tree in her seductive perfumed holiness. But you cannot. You are only a traveler. And then you are out of it and it is gone.

But you cherish the affair and yearn to walk that way again. What began with the mystery of fragrance has become a gateway.

שַׁעֲרֵי שָׁמַיִם

Shaarey Shamayim

Entrances *to* Holiness

מְלֹא כָל־הָאָרֶץ כְּבוֹדוֹ

"His Presence fills the whole world"

Isaiah 6:3

כד/24

Entrances to holiness are everywhere.
The possibility of ascent is all the time.
Even at unlikely times and through unlikely places.
There is no place on earth without the Presence.

Numbers
Rabba
12.4

אֵין מָקוֹם פָּנוּי בָּאָרֶץ מִן הַשְׁכִינָה

כה/25

Jacob, our father, was on the run. With only a rock for a
pillow. In what he thought was some God forsaken
wilderness. Until he had the dream.
"Surely the Holy One Himself, must have been in this
very place and I didn't even know it!" And then he was
afraid.

Genesis
28:16-17

אָכֵן יֵשׁ יְהֹנָה בַּמָּקוֹם הַזֶּה וְאָנֹכִי לֹא יָדָעְתִּי וַיִּירָא

He said, "How awesome is this place. This is none other
than God's house and here I am at the very doorway to
heaven!"

Genesis
28:17

וַיֹּאמַר מַה־נּוֹרָא הַמָּקוֹם הַזֶּה אֵין זֶה כִּי אִם־בֵּית אֱלֹהִים וְזֶה שַׁעַר
הַשָּׁמָיִם

In another place we read of how the Holy One chose a
common insignificant thorn bush. As if to teach us that
nothing is beneath being a gateway to the Most High. He

could have summoned mountains or oceans or the heavens themselves. But instead He "opened" a bush.

וַיַּרְא וְהִנֵּה הַסְּנֶה בֹּעֵר בָּאֵשׁ וְהַסְּנֶה אֵינֶנּוּ אֻכָּל

Exodus 3:2

And [Moses] looked and behold the bush was on fire but the bush was not consumed.

How long must someone look at a burning bush to know whether or not it is being consumed? Certainly longer than most people look at anything. Longer, in other words, than you need to. More than to see it. Or to use it. Long enough to see if it will be for you an Entrance. Such a man was Moses, our teacher. And likewise, anyone who is able to gaze on a place long enough without being distracted.

Once there was a man who could enter higher worlds merely by drawing a circle in the earth and standing within it. "I can do nothing very well except draw circles and stand in them," he would say. "But the circles are as perfect as are humanly possible and I can station myself within them without distraction." And so the Holy One would come out of hiding. Such a man was Honi, the circle drawer.

". . . מֶה עָשָׂה עָג עוּגָה וְעָמַד בְּתוֹכָהּ וְאָמַר לְפָנָיו רבש"ע

Taanit 19a

אֵינִי זָז מִכַּאן עַד שֶׁתְּרַחֵם עַל בָּנֶיךָ וְהִתְחִילוּ גְּשָׁמִים מְנַטְּפִין"

In a wilderness. Through a bush. From a circle. Nothing is beneath the dignity of being selected as an entrance.

"Remove your shoes from your feet for the place upon which you are standing is holy ground."

שַׁל־נְעָלֶיךָ מֵעַל רַגְלֶיךָ כִּי הַמָּקוֹם אֲשֶׁר אַתָּה עוֹמֵד עָלָיו אַדְמַת־קֹדֶשׁ הוּא

Exodus 3:5

Not that ground then. But this ground now. Not Jacob or Moses or Honi. But you who are reading these lines.

You do not have to go anywhere to raise yourself. You do not have to become anyone other than yourself to find entrances. You are already there. You are already everything you need to be. Entrances are everywhere and all the time.

There is no man who does not have his hour and no thing that does not have its place.

Avot
4:3

אֵין לְךָ אָדָם שֶׁאֵין לוֹ שָׁעָה וְאֵין לְךָ דָּבָר שֶׁאֵין לוֹ מָקוֹם

כו/26

Oh blessed candles, I remember how on one early dark November before-dinner-time evening, I saw you, slid through you and behind you, took you with me, and was blessed to recite the blessing . . . *who has brought us to this precious moment.* וְהִגִּיעָנוּ לַזְּמַן הַזֶּה . . .

Daily
Prayer-
book

כז/27

The First Snow

One day I visited my daughter's first grade class. There was a teacher and her assistant and myself. And eighteen souls who have been present for but six winters. The air hung with a November chill. The children were work/playing in four or five groups, when the mist outside turned imperceptibly into snowflakes. "Look! It's snowing outside!" one shouted. "Winter is here!" And the groups crumbled as their members ran to the windows. No need for daily prayer here. Or for the proper blessing on seeing nature's wonders for the first time. Not for them. But for me!

Praised are You, O Holy wonderful Lord, Master of the universe, who makes things like this.

בָּרוּךְ אַתָּה יְיָ אֱלֹהֵינוּ מֶלֶךְ הָעוֹלָם עֹשֶׂה מַעֲשֵׂה בְרֵאשִׁית

Daily Prayer-book

"Quick Daddy! Help me on with my coat. We're going outside!" And I stood at the window watching the snow fall on my little girl. There are places children go that grown-ups can only observe from afar.

כח/28

The Shortest Proper Blessing

One Shabbos dinner both children were ill. We spent more time trying to pacify them than on making a holy meal. And, as so often happens at such times, the end of the meal with its sharing and singing and blessing simply disintegrated. I was left alone at the table without even enough dedication to sing the final blessing. It was then that I remembered that a friend had pointed out to me the shortest ritually sufficient concluding prayer. He had even written it down on a card that was somewhere in the study. I resolved to say its five Aramaic words if only I could find it.

[51]

Once I located it, I realized that I had mispelled a word and that I wasn't sure of the meaning of two others. First I had to search out the phrase in Tractate *Berakhot*. Then I had to look up the words, which by now had become very important. Now as it happens, God gave me a good hand and I am something of a calligrapher. I decided to write the blessing in as beautiful a script as I could. I convinced myself that the prohibition against writing on the Sabbath had not been intended to thwart so personal a mode of thanks. Not only would I fix the words in my mind but I might, on this confused evening, offer the work of my hands in gratitude.

It was one of those beautiful sunset evenings. The long shadows of the trees gently blowing in the evening breeze. And just as I made the last dot I became aware that someone was in the room. I looked up expecting to find Karen or one of the kids (who are very good at sneaking up on you). But no one was there. Just a presence. And the fading shadows.

Blessed be the compassionate One, Master of this bread.

Berachot
40b

בְּרִיךְ רַחֲמָנָא מָרֵיה דְּהַאי פִּיתָא

כט/29

The Museum Entrance

We once spent a week in Holland and during our visit to Amsterdam stayed at a place called the Museum Hotel. From there we toured the city and countryside and saw what I thought were all the sights. From my garret window I even drew pictures of the great gabled building across the street. And from one of those sketches I did one of the better paintings I have ever done. I gave that oil to one of my teachers and when I last saw it, it was hanging in his front hallway. But it was only a few years ago that I learned that our hotel drew its name from the Rijks Museum and that I had painted a picture of one of the great painting halls of the world. For even though, I must have passed its door tens of times, I did not know I was passing the entrance to the Rijks Museum. I guess I was not then ready.

ﬡ/30

But how is it then that some things and places seem to be holy while others seem hopelessly profane. Surely there is a difference between goblets of wine and glasses of beer or Jerusalem and Las Vegas. This comes about not because of anything intrinsic to the things or the places but rather because of people and memories.

Because of people, for they try to hoard spiritual power like any other kind of power. Unaware, alas, that such power can only be shared but never possessed.

And because of memories, some things and places carry within them more memories of ascent than others. They are easily opened so that even one who is unsuspecting might accidently slip through them to higher worlds.

לא/31

Graves on the Side of a Hill

Once we made our way down the hundreds of steps leading to the old cemetery of Safed. High in the Galilean hills, the town was for centuries the center of Judaism's greatest mystical revival. Buried on the side of the mountain lies Rabbi Isaac Luria, the Lion, the Ari, creator of Lurianic Kabbala. So many visitors have come to light a candle here and deposit a pebble that the place is covered with stones and melted wax. And scrawled notes and crumpled prayers. And except for the unending breeze from the valleys below, there is stillness. Next to Luria is Alkabetz, author of *Lecha Dodi*, the great Sabbath love hymn. On the other side is Joseph Karo, author of the *Shulchan Aruch*, the great Code of Law. It was here that we found ourselves. Although we were not sure why we had come. And then after a few moments, we understood.

The memories of a place become a part of it. Places and things never forget what they have been witnesses to and vehicles of and entrances for. What has happened there happened nowhere else. Like ghosts who can neither forget what they have seen nor leave the place where they saw it, such are the memories tied to places of ascent. Temples. Trees. Melodies. Objects. Words. Whatever they have witnessed is chiseled into their substance.

לב/32

Is it possible to sense that some awesome ascent began in some place long after it had happened? A great oak like *Elon Mamre* of the book of Genesis grows rigid in the September sun. How old is it really? Under it some sought shelter, perhaps were conceived, or perhaps died and were buried. The events continue to occur. Without end or beginning. They never stop happening. If someone ever enters a higher world through some thing, then they eternally ascend through that thing. It only appears to us to be of finite duration. For this reason it is not surprising that some things and places do seem holy. But it is not because of them. Only what they "remember." The Western Wall has been, for so many, for so long, a place of ascent, that it is more likely a door. Even casual tourists are often astonished to encounter "its" holiness. The stones of the wall are smooth from the centuries of hands who have caressed them. The visitors have left more than their tangible traces — the stones and their paper petitions. They have left a residue that is immeasurable and invisible.

לג/33

And then other people come who would sell us tickets to the holy places. Who perhaps once and perhaps still, but

probably never, were themselves graced to witness or themselves to ascend higher. Culture and organized religion conspire to trick us into believing that entrances to holiness are only at predictable times and prearranged places. (Sometimes they are right.) Otherwise people would not pay their dues. And most of us professional holy people would have to set out again in search of the Nameless One.

לך/34

The cycle alternates between grand cathedrals and meditation amidst the trees of the forest. When people become convinced that the places and the things are themselves holy or that only some people have the spiritual power, then it is time once more to set out for the fields and rediscover the fundamental truth: Entrances to holiness are everywhere and all the time.

4

עֲצַת הַשֵׁם

Atzat HaShem

The Hands *of* Heaven

עֲצַת יְהֹוָה הִיא תָקוּם

"God's plan will come to be."

Proverbs 19:21

לה /35

Life is inescapably filled with meaning. That is because the whole thing is prearranged. We have no more freedom than an oak tree. That is, we are free to be who we are or free to pretend that we are someone else. But we are not free to be someone else.

And this is the meaning of meaning: Being connected with something that is itself connected with something. Being part of a constellation of parts that is itself part of an even greater scheme. Or, in other words, that the notion of parts is in truth, a convenience we perpetrate so as to permit us not having to fathom the consequences of our most trivial acts. Nothing is entirely separate. No one acts with caprice. The Holy One is always involved.

לו /36

Freedom, in the way most people use the word, is only an excuse to insist on moral culpability which is only an excuse to pretend that the social good we do is from fear of punishment — instead of saying that we do everything we do because we want to. Which is the same as saying that we have no alternative. No alternative except one.

THE HANDS OF HEAVEN

We are free to be aware of the significance of each moment. To understand our destiny. Or to avoid it.

All is in the hands of Heaven save the fear of Heaven.

הַכֹּל בִּידֵי שָׁמַיִם חוּץ מִיִּרְאַת שָׁמָיִם

*Berachot
33b*

To fear Heaven is to search for the holy intention that might be realized by our every act or discerned everywhere round about us.

לז/37

Ramban (Nachmanides) teaches us that *no man has any portion in the Torah of Moses, our teacher, until he understands that every one of our words and encounters, both in private and in public, are miracles and cannot be attributed merely to some natural capricious order of the universe.*

... שֶׁכֻּלָּם נִסִּים אֵין בָּהֶם טֶבַע וּמִנְהָגוֹ שֶׁל עוֹלָם בֵּין בָּרַבִּים בֵּין
בַּיָּחִיד ...

*End of
parashat
Bo*

And so words, actions, feelings, lives, and history have come from something and are destined to go to something. Coming forth from a shared seed of the past. Setting out for a common fulfillment in the future. Each one has a definite purpose. Each one assumes meaning — from the greatest to the least, are all part of the plan. And for this reason the great purpose can be revealed to each of us everywhere. Everything comes to teach us something about God's plan and therefore, our destiny.

לח/38

There is a story told of Reb Elimelech of Lizensk. It was said of him that he had gone beyond his ego to the extent that he was no longer conscious of himself as a discrete entity. And because of this, he perpetually merged with the One of the universe.

People would follow his carriage but Elimelech could never understand why. He would ask his coachman why all the people were trailing behind and the coachman would explain about how the people wanted to follow after wisdom and holiness. And then Elimelech would decide that they were doing the right thing by following after the carriage. And he would get out and join the people following the empty carriage.

Eser Tzach- tzochot I. Berger Piotrkov, 1910 p. 19

וְכַאֲשֶׁר בָּא הרר"א עִם הָעֲגָלָה שֶׁלוֹ חוּץ לָעִיר יָרַד גַּם הוּא מֵהָעֲגָלָה שֶׁלוֹ לְבֵין הָאֲנָשִׁים שֶׁהָלְכוּ לְלַוּוֹתוֹ ... וּכְנִרְאֶה שֶׁהֵם מְלַוִּים אֶת הָעֲגָלָה וְלֹא אֶת הרר"א ...

In another place we read that the Kotzker taught that "One who is too filled with himself has no room for the Holy One." Which is another way of saying that God only inhabits empty carriages. And that true holy men know this and that is why they get out of the carriage.

Now the way to this way of being is not through abnegation of oneself but rather through the realization that because one can do nothing else anyway, the carriage has been empty all along.

לט/39

As we read in Isaiah *For My plans are not your plans,
. . . For as the rain and snow come from heaven, and
return not there but soaks the earth, and makes it bring
forth vegetation, yielding seed for sowing and bread for
eating so it is with the word that comes out of My
mouth, it does not come back to me with its task un-
done. . . .*

כִּי לֹא מַחְשְׁבוֹתַי מַחְשְׁבוֹתֵיכֶם . . . כִּי כַּאֲשֶׁר יֵרֵד הַגֶּשֶׁם וְהַשֶּׁלֶג
מִן־הַשָּׁמַיִם וְשָׁמָּה לֹא יָשׁוּב כִּי אִם־הִרְוָה אֶת־הָאָרֶץ וְהוֹלִידָהּ
וְהִצְמִיחָהּ וְנָתַן זֶרַע לַזֹּרֵעַ וְלֶחֶם לָאֹכֵל כֵּן יִהְיֶה דְבָרִי אֲשֶׁר יֵצֵא
מִפִּי לֹא־יָשׁוּב אֵלַי רֵיקָם

*Isaiah
55:
8,10,11*

And because we understand this (sometimes) we write
the abbreviation *Bet Hay* or *Bet Samech Dalet* above
written ventures. Which means that it is only attempted
"with the help of God." Or we whisper before any plan
we set, *Im Yertza HaShem.* "If it be the intention of God
. . ."

מ/40

We call two lovers soon to be wed his intended and her
intended. Without naming the Nameless One who it was
that intended.

And Isaac went out to meditate in the fields at twilight
וַיֵּצֵא יִצְחָק לָשׂוּחַ בַּשָּׂדֶה לִפְנוֹת עָרֶב

*Genesis
24:63*

and when he looked up he saw Rebecca, for the first time, "And Isaac went out" to encounter one who was intended for him.

When you first fell in love, confessed to each other that this romance must now build a home, there was a moment when you understood that the intention was not yours alone. There was a moment when to say anything less than that "since the creation of the universe it was written that this woman and this man would stand under this tree and agree to build a home together" — would be blasphemy. That which the old ones call in Yiddish *Ba'shert* "meant to be," is not a lessening of one's "freedom," but rather when encountered personally, a heightened freedom. A rising to one's destiny. And what had before seemed free now, seems shadowed momentarily in unawareness. And this is true of moments of ascent. We understand that there is a kind of freedom and moral responsibility that goes beyond everyday illusions of free will which is called doing what you are intended to do. Of course one can evade even this. But not forever. Sooner or later, in one lifetime or another, each soul must accomplish its intended task.

We read in the Midrash that *the Holy One spends His time arranging meetings and marriages. He takes this one who is unsuspecting from one end of the world and pairs them with that one who is unwilling from the other end of the world.*

הַקָּדוֹשׁ־בָּרוּךְ־הוּא יוֹשֵׁב וּמְזַוֵּג בְּעַל כָּרְחָן וְקוֹשֵׁר קוֹלָר בְּצַוַּאר זֶה
וּמְבִיאוֹ מִסּוֹף הָעוֹלָם וּמְזַוֵּג לָזוֹ בְּסוֹף הָעוֹלָם

Tanhuma
Ki Tisa
5

מא/41

Rabbi Shmuel bar Nachman explained the words of Jeremiah:

For I have known all along what I have intended for you, says God, a destiny of peace and not of evil, to give you a future and a hope.

כִּי אָנֹכִי יָדַעְתִּי אֶת־הַמַּחֲשָׁבֹת אֲשֶׁר אָנֹכִי חֹשֵׁב עֲלֵיכֶם נְאֻם־יְהוָה מַחְשְׁבוֹת שָׁלוֹם וְלֹא לְרָעָה לָתֵת לָכֶם אַחֲרִית וְתִקְוָה

Jeremiah 29:11

Rabbi Shmuel suggested that this refers to the strange events of Genesis 38.

The last four *parashot* of the book of Genesis (chapters 37-50) comprise a complete literary unit which tells of how the Jewish people came to settle in Egypt. All the necessary elements of the plot are present in the novella and, with one very odd exception, nothing seems extraneous to the unfolding story. Chapter 38 simply does not appear to fit. At the height of the action, with Joseph sold to a caravan, his brothers having deceived their father, his father mourning Joseph's death, Judah leaves the scene and (after some very complicated familial and sexual adventures) fathers Zerah and Perez. Whereupon, we return to the story of Joseph in Egypt.

Perhaps, hints Rabbi Shmuel, the explanation can be found by tracing the genealogy of Perez. When we do, we discover that he was destined to be a distant grandparent of King David and therefore of the Messiah. Now

the hidden divine intention becomes apparent. Here at precisely this moment when all seemed lost did the Holy One have Judah, without his own knowledge, step out of the narrative and tend to the line of the redeemer. While everyone else was consumed with their own plans, *the Holy One too was tending to the light of the Messiah.*

Genesis Rabba 85.1

וְהַקָדוֹשׁ בָּרוּךְ הוּא הָיָה עוֹסֵק בּוֹרֵא אוֹרוֹ שֶׁל מֶלֶךְ הַמָּשִׁיחַ

As we read in Isaiah: *Before she had the pangs of childbirth, she gave birth.* בְּטֶרֶם תָּחִיל יָלָדָה

Isaiah 66:7

Even before the first pharoah was conceived, the final redeemer was prepared.

The Hebrew Bible only knows of one way. That which God has intended shall come to pass. Usually we only sense the great events as being intended, as "having come to pass." But surely it is so for each couple who agree to build a home. And perhaps for each letter of each word of each utterance.

At the end of the Joseph epic, Joseph consoles his brothers still contriving and conspiring to manipulate without "becoming aware" of their own destiny,

"Do not be afraid, am I God? For while you [thought you] were planning evil against me God was planning good . . ."

Genesis 50:19-20

אַל תִּירָאוּ כִּי הֲתַחַת אֱלֹהִים אָנִי וְאַתֶּם חֲשַׁבְתֶּם עָלַי רָעָה אֱלֹהִים חֲשָׁבָהּ לְטֹבָה

מב/42

The Balcony

They are building a balcony in our synagogue's prayer hall. It will not be for seating; it will be for the library. A merging of prayer and study. A long overdue return to that ancient Jewish synthesis of prayer and study. It is still incomplete. There is a plywood floor and only roughed-in stairs all somehow hanging on this great steel beam. The workmen were careful to barricade the stairway and set bold signs of warning. But one Shabbos morning for the concluding *Aleynu* prayer, we stormed the barricades and climbed the stairs. "Bowing our head and bending our knees" a full story above the only floor we had until this moment ever known. None of us were at all prepared for the simple astonishment bestowed on those who are able to rise high enough to gaze down on where they had once stood, once prayed, once believed was the highest they would every go. Some of us even dared to look even higher toward what we would never again call the ceiling.

מג/43

The higher one's awareness goes
The more more things increase in importance.
It becomes harder and harder to imagine their presence

As merely chance.
Until from the highest rungs
Everything is seen. Everything is understood.
Everything in its place.
Even this moment of heightened awareness
Intended to be just now.

There is no struggle or anxiety in any of this.
Only seeing with our eyes and hearing with our ears.
For in truth, you can do nothing save what is intended.
There is only avoiding or awareness.

5

מַלְאֲכֵי עֶלְיוֹן

Malachey Elyon

Messengers *of the* Most High

וַיֹּאמֶר לָמָּה זֶּה תִּשְׁאַל לִשְׁמִי . . .

''And he said, 'Why do you ask my name?' ''

Genesis 32:30

מד /44

The Hebrew word for angel is *malach*. Which also means messenger. One who is sent.

Not cherubic creatures who adorn architecture, valentines, and fantasy. They can be anyone who is sent. Just as anyone who is sent can be an angel. It is required only that there be an errand. One message.
One angel never performs two missions just as two angels never go on one mission.

Genesis Rabba 50:2

אֵין מַלְאָךְ אֶחָד עוֹשֶׂה שְׁתֵּי שְׁלִיחוֹת וְלֹא שְׁנֵי מַלְאָכִים עוֹשִׂים שְׁלִיחוּת אֶחָת

There is one great difference between people chosen to be God's messengers and earthly messengers. While those on errands of this world almost always know that they are sent and where and why, people chosen to be messengers of the Most High rarely even know that they are His messengers. Unsuspecting and unaware. Consumed by their own plans and itineraries. Busy at work on their own schemes. God is already sending them somewhere else.

I do not know how many times in one's life one is also a messenger. But for everyone it is at least once. One to whom it is given to know that their errand is completed is blessed and rare. Not so for most of us.

Remember only that you are not always going where you are going for the reasons you think you are.

מה/45

... *When the angels are sent (as messengers) by His word they are changed into winds, and when they minister before Him they are changed into fire, as it is said, "Who makes His angels into winds; His ministers, a flaming fire."*

Psalm 104:4

כְּשֶׁהֵן נִשְׁלָחִין בְּדַבְּרוֹ נַעֲשִׂין רוּחוֹת וּכְשֶׁהֵן מְשָׁרְתִים פָּנָיו נַעֲשִׂין שֶׁל אֵשׁ שֶׁנֶּאֱמַר עֹשֶׂה מַלְאָכָיו רוּחוֹת מְשָׁרְתָיו אֵשׁ לֹהֵט

Pirke deRabbi Eliezer 4

What is it like to stand into the wind?
Pretty much like talking to anyone.
What is it like to speak to a messenger of the Most High?
Like standing into the wind.

מו/46

There must have been a time when you entered a room and met someone and after a while you understood that unknown to either of you there was a reason you had met. You had changed the other or he had changed you. By some word or deed or just by your presence the errand had been completed. Then perhaps you were a little bewildered or humbled and grateful. And it was over.

Each lifetime is the pieces of a jigsaw puzzle.
For some there are more pieces.
For others the puzzle is more difficult to assemble.

Some seem to be born with a nearly completed puzzle.
And so it goes.
Souls going this way and that
Trying to assemble the myriad parts.

But know this. No one has within themselves
All the pieces to their puzzle.
Like before the days when they used to seal
jigsaw puzzles in cellophane. Insuring that
All the pieces were there.

Everyone carries with them at least one and probably
Many pieces to someone else's puzzle.
Sometimes they know it.
Sometimes they don't.

And when you present your piece
Which is worthless to you,
To another, whether you know it or not,
Whether they know it or not,
You are a messenger from the Most High.

מז/47

We read in Genesis that *The Lord appeared [to Abraham] by the terebinths of Mamre; He was sitting at the entrance of the tent at the heat of the day. Looking up, he saw three men [messengers] standing near him. . .*

Genesis 18:1-2

וַיֵּרָא אֵלָיו יְהֹוָה בְּאֵלֹנֵי מַמְרֵא וְהוּא יֹשֵׁב פֶּתַח־הָאֹהֶל כְּחֹם הַיּוֹם.
וַיִּשָּׂא עֵינָיו וַיַּרְא וְהִנֵּה שְׁלֹשָׁה אֲנָשִׁים נִצָּבִים עָלָיו . . .

Benno Jacob, commenting on Abraham's intimacy with the Holy One observes that, "God appears to (Abraham) through three men; the closer a person's relationship to God, the more human is the form of God's manifestation."

The Zohar is even more explicit: *And indeed whenever the celestial spirits descend to earth, they clothe themselves in physical things and appear to men in human shape.*

וְלָא יִקְשֶׁה לָךְ הָאי דְּהָא וַדַּאי אִינוּן רוּחִין קַדִּישִׁין וּבְשַׁעֲתָא
דְּנַחְתֵּי לְעָלְמָא מִתְלַבְּשִׁין בְּאַוִּירִין וּבִיסוֹדֵי דְגוֹלְמִין וְאִתְחֲזוּ לִבְנֵי
נָשָׁא מַמָּשׁ כְּחֵיזוּ דְיוּקְנָא דִילְהוֹן . . .

Zohar
I
101a

מח/48

Another One's Tefilin

Tefilin are small black leather boxes containing bits of parchment on which are written prescribed paragraphs from the Torah. With leather straps they are bound . . . "for a sign upon thy hand and for frontlets between thine eyes" . . . upon the forehead and the arm each morning. It is an act of personal devotion and obedience to the Master. Now these days *Tefilin* are only regularly worn by observant traditional Jews. The rest of us wear them with less frequency in between which times we store these sacred utensils in the back of the drawer where we also keep our socks. I happen to have an idiosyncrasy when it comes to *Tefilin*. Whenever I travel

Deuter-
onomy
6:8

overnight, I carry my *Tefilin* with me. I tell myself that just in case the spirit should move me, or if I should feel spiritually weakened, I would have them with me. Well, what can I say, after maybe several dozen trips I still haven't put them on but a few times. Nevertheless I still carry them. I even suggested once that I had stumbled upon some new commandment. The commandment of carrying your *Tefilin* with you to hotel rooms.

Then, the other day, a dear friend told me that his mother had given away his set of *tefilin*. There were tears in his eyes when he told me.

And then I understood why I had carried my "unused" *tefilin* with me all this time. They weren't mine. I was only bringing them to their intended owner. "They must be yours," I said.

מט/49

One of the most important people in the Torah remains nameless. His name, if indeed he has one, is subservient to the task he was sent to perform. He is known only by his deed. Sent by the Most High from another world to alter the course of this one. He is literally *Deus Ex Machina*, a divine one, whose presence in the plot is awkwardly contrived. Some uninvited guest whose only function is to do one thing. And then, never to be heard from again. Perhaps he had an elaborate and full life. A constellation of intricate and interlocking relationships.

But so far as the Holy One is concerned he had but one moment. One task. Pressed into His service, who knows, perhaps against his will or even without his knowledge. A messenger who does not know he is a messenger. An actor with a one-line walk-on part. Unnamed in the program.

The Torah only calls him *ish*, "someone." Yet without him the children of Israel would never have stayed in Egypt. Never been freed. Never crossed the sea. Indeed, never have come into being as a people.

In the final chapters of Genesis we read in the Joseph saga of a favored and spoiled son. A boy whose bragging and dreams earn him the wrath of his brothers who sold him to a caravan bound for Egypt and what they hoped would be oblivion. A boy whose gift as a dream interpreter set him second only to Pharaoh himself. A boy who acquired such power that he was able to manipulate his eleven brothers and father into coming down to Egypt and ultimately settling there. Clearly, the Torah means to teach us that it is all the doing of the Holy One. Event after event has the unmistakable mark of divine contrivance. But of all the scenes chronicling our descent into Egypt none seems more superfluous and dramatically unnecessary than the scene in Shechem.

Joseph's Father sent him to find out how things are going with his brothers whom they both believe are tending the flocks in Shechem. But when he arrives there, they have already left. And we read:

. . . And a man came upon him wandering in the fields. The man asked him, "What are you looking for?" He

answered, "I am looking for my brothers. Could you tell me where they are pasturing?" The man said, "They have gone from here, for I heard them say: Let us go to Dothan."

Genesis
37:15-17

וַיִּמְצָאֵהוּ אִישׁ וְהִנֵּה תֹעֶה בַּשָּׂדֶה וַיִּשְׁאָלֵהוּ הָאִישׁ לֵאמֹר מַה־תְּבַקֵּשׁ: וַיֹּאמֶר אֶת־אַחַי אָנֹכִי מְבַקֵּשׁ הַגִּידָה־נָא לִי אֵיפֹה הֵם רֹעִים: וַיֹּאמֶר הָאִישׁ נָסְעוּ מִזֶּה כִּי שָׁמַעְתִּי אֹמְרִים נֵלְכָה דֹּתָיְנָה

Ramban teaches *that the "man" was a messenger. And that this odd scene has not been for nothing.*

Ramban
on Genesis
37:15

"... כִּי הָאֲנָשִׁים הָאֵלֶּה הֵם מַלְאָכִים שֶׁלֹּא עַל חִנָּם הָיָה כָּל הַסִּפּוּר הַזֶּה"

Indeed were it not for the man who "happened" to find Joseph wandering in the fields, he would have returned home. Never been sold into slavery. Never brought his family down to Egypt. The Jewish people would have never become slaves. And indeed there could have been no Jewish people at all.

We are only *ish*, someone. No more and no less than the unnamed stranger of the empty pastures of Shechem, without whose one line, "I heard them say, 'Let us go to Dothan . . .' ", the Holy One's intention could not be realized.

נ/50

And so we understand that ordinary people are messengers of the Most High. They go about their tasks in holy anonymity. Often, even unknown to themselves.

Yet, if they had not been there, if they had not said what they said or did what they did, it would not be the way it is now. We would not be the way we are now. Never forget that you too yourself may be a messenger. Perhaps even one whose errand extends over several lifetimes.

6

גִּלְגּוּלִים

Gilgulim

Circles *of* Return

כִּי אֶת־אֲשֶׁר יֶשְׁנוֹ פֹּה עִמָּד הַיּוֹם
לִפְנֵי יְהוָה אֱלֹהֵינוּ
וְאֵת אֲשֶׁר אֵינֶנּוּ פֹּה עִמָּנוּ הַיּוֹם

"With those who are standing here with us today
in the presence of the Lord our God
and with those who are not here with us today."

Deuteronomy 29:14

נא/51

Everything returns. Comes back to that which it was. This is not futility. It is fulfillment.

A generation goes and a generation comes. The earth remains forever. And the sun rises and the sun sets and glides back to where it rises.

Ecclesiastes 1:4-5

דּוֹר הֹלֵךְ וְדוֹר בָּא וְהָאָרֶץ לְעוֹלָם עֹמָדֶת וְזָרַח הַשֶּׁמֶשׁ וּבָא הַשֶּׁמֶשׁ וְאֶל־מְקוֹמוֹ שׁוֹאֵף זוֹרֵחַ הוּא שָׁם

All the people
In all the cars on
All the roads
That ever were or
Ever will be
Are on the same clover-leaf.

Only none of the exit ramps have tangents. They only lead to another ramp. Which is itself a circle. It appears as though you are getting off, but you are only getting on. And this getting on is itself another exit.

And of course it is really only one circle. And the circle is actually a sphere. Space and time are most certainly curved. In a perfect curve. In the same circle. In one sphere. The first man and the last man, they are present now.

And religious time knows this. Just as religious ritual intends to sustain the circle of return. Just as religious myth means to remember it. To keep it ever in our awareness.

נב/52

The Same Tree

When I was little I made a painting of a tree. It was going to be a landscape but I lost interest and now somewhere in the folio of my childhood drawings is one of a completed tree surrounded by white watercolor paper. I had completely forgotten the whole business.

Then this morning I caught myself gazing at the tree I had once before "seen" and painted, only now it was growing beside the driveway.

נג/53

There are two ways of experiencing the flow of time. In contemporary secular time, time is infinitely and irreversably linear. It is without beginning or end. And since no two moments ever coincide, each minute, day, week, and year must have its own unique number.

In religious time, on the other hand, the flow of time began with God's word and likewise will end with His word. And within these two termini there are identical circles of time. Some are larger, some smaller. There are

weeks, each ending with a Sabbath. But every Sabbath is identical to every other Sabbath even as they are all like the Sabbath on which "God rested from all his work that He had done." Holy time does not march on. Once the candles are lit there is no "next" Shabbos. Within each week eternity recapitulates itself. The Jewish people are freed from Egypt. Receive the Torah. Wander the wilderness. For this reason a Jewish child is not named until the eighth day — only then it has lived! Taking Rosenzweig's division of Sabbath time we discover that on Friday evening we are freed from Egypt/slavery of the week. On Sabbath morning we receive the Torah/read its weekly portion. And at Havdalla we wander forever in the wilderness (cf. Mircea Eliade *The Myth of the Eternal Return* Princeton University Press 1954).

In another circle there are years. But they are all the same. It is unimportant, for instance, to know the exact date for when the great exodus from Egypt took place. The going out from slavery reoccurs every year on Pesach. It occurred even before the secular going out from Egypt ever was. Before there was an Egypt — the Jews went forth from Egypt. Once the Seder begins there is no "last" Pesach. There is only this one. Said Rabbi Judah ben R. Shalour, *There is no before and there is no after in the Torah* אֵין מֻקְדָּם וּמְאֻחָר בַּתּוֹרָה

Midrash Tanhuma Teruma 8

There is no before and no after in the unconscious either. Then is now. Now is then.

And there are cycles of sabbatical years. And larger cycles of sabbatical - sabbatical years or Jubilee years. But they are all the same.

So you see, secular time looks like this:

While spiritual time looks like this:

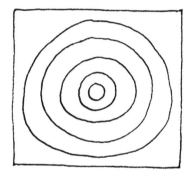

And since every moment that has occurred is also occurring and will occur again, we cannot graphically indicate any particular moment. For even the end of time and the beginning of time are in some sense identical with one another.

Already science and mathematics have begun to rediscover this: "Space near a collapsing star is curved by the gravitational field of the star in the same way a rubber sheet could be curved by . . . a heavy object placed on it . . . The eventual fate of this curved space was first described by Einstein and Rosen. Suprisingly, they found that space-time eventually opens up into a

second universe." (William J. Kaufman III, "Pathways through The Universe-Black holes, Worm holes, and White holes" in *Mercury*, 1974, March/June, p. 29. Also from *Relativity and Cosmology*, Harper & Row, 1973, chaps. 6 and 7.)

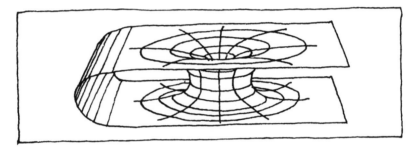

First the "plane of space-time" is flattened out so as to make the original "hole" more like a curved "pipeline."

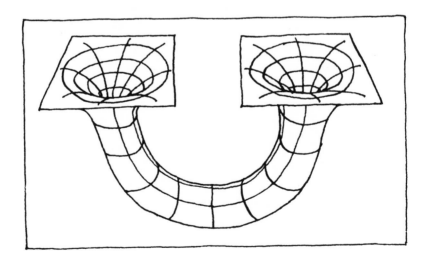

Then the plane can fold even more until what remains is a circle so that the sought-after distant time-space becomes always one with this time-space.

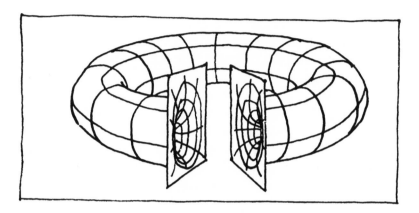

Everything returns.

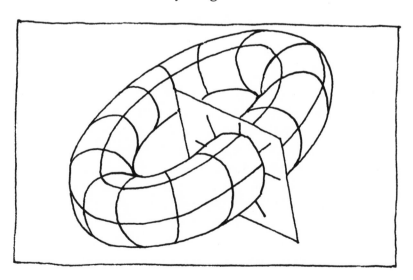

נד/54

Not only does time turn back upon itself in great circles
but also things of space. From galaxies to individual
cells, everything participates in great cycles of return. To
be sure, sometimes the orbit is so large that it appears to
be straight. But sooner or later it will return. The
molecules that form this moment will reassemble once
again for another sacred convocation. Even as our souls
are destined to reappear in one incarnation after another.
Even as the first man will himself be re-formed by all of
us together. And at that time will he be known as the last
man.

נה/55

Death is the amnesia separating one life experience from
another. It is only the enemy for those who seek to hold
on to this world in order to control and possess. For them
even the quest for immortality is but another way toward
acquiring. Of such ones it is said that they are dead even
while they are alive. Surrounded by lifeless possessions
or lives that they seek to possess. It is this most common
and universal way to escape death that is the real source
of evil and the amnesia separating one life experience
from another. Not so for those who share their lives with
others. For them death is simply the final opportunity

for giving. To such individuals is granted the awareness of the circles in which their souls participate. "I wish you would not come to me so soon," they say as death approaches, "but I have been ready for you since I first became aware. Living each day as if it were my last." For such ones, the awareness of life times having come before is heightened. Their lessons clearer. Their tasks ahead more defined.

The aware rise in spirals to ever higher rungs of awareness in each lifetime. Until finally they will have been through and been everyone and everything. They reach out to death and inquire "now where?" Because once they were both beggar and rich, they understand. Because at one time in their past, they lived on every rung of being — human and animal. And through their own light they try to share their awareness. For they know that we are each different fragmentary manifestations of the Holy One Himself. And that the ultimate unification cannot occur until every single soul has become fully aware. Not until the wickedest person — the one with the most amnesia — seeks holiness instead, will the last part of the last man be realized.

נו/56

On Burying a Dead Squirrel on Erev Kol Nidre

Of all the times, the one just before the sunset that begins Yom Kippur, is the most anxious. Will the "turn-

ing" be complete? Will my sermon be worthy of my students and of their needs and of the hour? Will the prayers be answered? Will we live or die? And if I am not careful I will become so consumed with such cosmic concerns that I will neglect my family.

One Erev Kol Nidre we were driving home and in the road in front of a nearby vacant lot lay the body of a dead squirrel. So many of them die at this time of year — automobile fatalities — that the highway department can not possibly get to them. The animals get careless about gathering food for the winter. The unwritten law seems to be that if it's in front of your house, you bury it. But if it's on ownerless property *(If someone is found slain . . .*

Deuter- *lying in an open field . . . They [the elders] shall say "our*
onomy *hands did not shed this blood . . .''* כִּי־יִמָּצֵא חָלָל
21:1,7 *. . .*) . . . נֹפֵל בַּשָּׂדֶה . . . וְאָמְרוּ יָדֵינוּ לֹא שָׁפְכוּ אֶת־הַדָּם הַזֶּה) the corpse is likely to disintegrate beneath the unending stream of automobile tires.

Noa who was then five and Zack who was three were very worried by all this. They knew what I pretended to be too busy to remember: that the animal must be buried. And apparently this *mitzvah* had been given for us to do.

So we got the shovel and walked back down the road. I dug a grave. Buried the squirrel. Covered it over with earth. The children found some stones to mark the place. And then they wanted to know "Where it goes?" It is obvious to them that something has been buried but that also (even for an anonymous squirrel) something has not. It is clear to me now that this was how I was to get ready for this Yom Kippur.

Whatever it was that made this squirrel *this* squirrel now goes back to the Holy One. And God says (I conjecture for my children), "well little squirrel, you have been the best squirrel you could be and you have done what you needed to do and learned what you needed to learn. So now you can rest here with Me for a while and then I will send you back to be born of someone else. An oak tree, a bird, a stone — or perhaps even a person."

It's one of those holy stories that you can only tell in such a way that it could never have happened. But a story that nevertheless is true.

I wonder how people would treat the universe if they even sometimes believed in such transmigrations of souls. Would they be kinder to their world? To one another? To themselves?

And so the burial was over. It was almost time to have dinner and get dressed for services. A father carrying a shovel and two young children walking up the hill toward home.

זן/57

Three Short Visits

Evening

I have waited all these days for a visit from Luria. And now. *Erev Shabbos.* Sitting on the bed. Playing with the

little girl. Not Luria but Eliyahu himself comes! I am sorry, messenger. I am busy now. I pray you would come another time. When I'm not with the little girl. You see, it is very difficult for me to be with her and I do not trade such moments even for messages from the Most High.

Morning

I am driving to the synagogue. There is an insect on the glass. A kind of fly with spotted wings. I do not know if it is on the inside of the glass or the outside. I wave my hand. He does not fly away. You stupid bug. What's the matter with you. Inside or out, a bug should fly away from the hand of man. But the fly does not fly. My God. It must be Luria! "What are you doing here on my car while I'm making a left turn?" "I have come to make you aware that no creature is beneath the dignity of being a messenger of the Most High. That is all. It is enough that you understood for even a moment that I am Luria. Goodbye."

Afternoon

The next afternoon Karen and I are having lunch. On the window sill I see a bug twitching in the throes of death. Bugs live only a short time, you know. It is the same fly in whom the soul that was once also Luria resided. "You see," he seems to say, "now that I have completed my mission I die, so do not be sad. What other reasons for life or death could there be?" But I was sad and I said a silent *Kaddish* and carried the tiny body outside to the wind.

נח/58

Traces

In March the snows do not last long. No sooner have they fallen than a rain falls and it is as if the snow had never been. Late one Friday evening I walked home through such a snow. I had the universe to myself and that unequalled joy of making the only footprints in new snow. Occasionally, I turned around and walked backwards so I could watch the tracks that I had just created. Later that night it warmed up and rained and by the time I returned to the synagogue the next morning there was not a trace of white to be found. But as I walked back retracing my steps it was as if the footprints remained. Perhaps there are traces people leave behind them in space and time as they make their way through the universe. Traces that cannot be eradicated. Through kings and wars and volcanoes. Traces that tell all. Even though the snow has melted overnight.

נט/59

Eternal life is only awareness. Understanding that everything participates in circles of return. That everyone will be transfigured and reborn. Even a stone will become earth in which a tree will bear fruit to be

eaten by a child which will become the twinkle of an eye.
Everything will change. And the Holy One will meet
everything backstage, in between performances. He will
answer all our questions and show us all of eternity from
one end to the other.

A light is lit for the fetus above its head
And by it he looks and gazes from
One end of eternity to the other
As it is said, "When His lamp shone above my head."

Job
29:3

Yalkut
Shimoni
II,916

וְנֵר דָּלוּק לוֹ עַל רֹאשׁוֹ וְצוֹפֶה וּמַבִּיט מִסּוֹף הָעוֹלָם וְעַד סוֹפוֹ
שֶׁנֶּאֱמַר בְּהִלּוֹ נֵרוֹ עֲלֵי רֹאשִׁי

The Holy One appears when one thing ends and another
thing begins. A baby is born. A child becomes an adult.
An old person dies. One enters a room. One leaves a
room. One sets out on a journey. *Blessed may you be in*
your coming in and blessed may you be in your going
out.

Deuter-
onomy
28.6

בָּרוּךְ אַתָּה בְּבֹאֶךָ וּבָרוּךְ אַתָּה בְּצֵאתֶךָ

God is there. In the spaces in between. Reminding us
that we have all along been destined to live forever.
Ascending through ever higher spirals of awareness and
chambers of light. Allowing us to remember what has
gone before. Now we are able to hang onto the thread
that binds one life awareness to the next. Returning
finally and again beings of pure light.

ס/60

Know that there is a river.
It does not flow within any time or any space.
One who struggles to stay afloat in its holy cold waters
Is out of time and out of space.
For this reason
The ordinary rules are suspended.
Strange ancient ritual takes over,
Guiding those who must now pass
From one mode of being to the next.
And since every crossing requires some kind of death
  and rebirth,
There is, for one who lives to set foot on the far bank,
A great celebration.
Wine and cake. Dancing and laughing. Speeches and
  tears.
(After all, the Bar Mitzvah might have died.)

For this reason,
The parents of one to be circumcised/named,
The parents of and the child about to become a Bar/Bat
  Mitzvah,
The bride and the groom
And the family just prior to a funeral,
All agree and invariably
Make the same request in one way or another:
Please make it fast.

Not wishing to dwell within or savor
Or even understand their own
Or their loved one's encounter
With the frightening power of holiness.

The holy man is a sort of boatman,
A pilot on the holy river.
He does not himself understand about the river,
Nor can he predict its current or control its caprice.
He only knows the way to the other side,
About manoeuvering the boat,
And the strange ancient rituals.

הַשַּׁעַר הַשְּׁבִיעִי
THE SEVENTH GATE

7

הָאוֹר

HaOr

The Light *of* Awareness

אוֹתוֹ אוֹרָה שֶׁנִּבְרָא בַּיּוֹם הָרִאשׁוֹן
הָיָה אָדָם צוֹפֶה וּמַבִּיט מִסוֹף הָעוֹלָם וְעַד סוֹפוֹ

"By means of that light which was created on the
first day man was able to gaze and behold eternity
from one end to the other."

Pesikta Rabbati 23:6

סא /61

Moses and Elijah — they are the same man.

Pesikta Rabbati 4.2

"... מֹשֶׁה וְאֵלִיָהוּ שָׁוִין זֶה לָזֶה בְּכָל דָּבָר"

Separated only by generations, their situations and their soul-solutions are identical. They participate in the same archetype. They are shoots from one branch: Humanity. They are you and I. Ones to whom the light is shown.

Moses was the first of all the prophets; Elijah was (will be) the last. Moses redeemed us from Egyptian slavery. And Elijah will redeem us from life that struggles against death. They both gathered Israel about a mountain: Sinai and Carmel. Both were once the only ones who had not deserted the Holy One either for the calf or for Baal. And so they were away forty days and forty nights and came to the mountain of God: Horeb-Sinai. And God hid each of them in a cleft-cave of the rock that had been waiting for them since before the creation was completed.

Pesachim 54a

"... מְעָרָה שֶׁעָמַד בּוֹ מֹשֶׁה וְאֵלִיָהוּ ..."

And it was here that each man received one needle-thin beam of light — which was apparently all either one of them could withstand or that God meant to share.

Megilah 19b

אִילְמָלֵי נִשְׁתַּיֵּיר בִּמְעָרָה שֶׁעָמַר בָּהּ מֹשֶׁה וְאֵלִיָהוּ כִּמְלֹא נֶקֶב מַחַט סִרְקִית לֹא הָיוּ יְכוֹלִין לַעֲמֹד מִפְּנֵי הָאוֹרָה

And, thus impregnated with this awareness, each left the cleft-cave of the rock.

[94]

For God was not in wind or in the quake or in the fire. Just a whispering sound of breathing out heard in the darkness of some cleft-cave in the rock. And the thin ray of light.

The cave might be the womb of creation. Mother earth. The shaft of light might be the fertile seed. Father God. And the one in the cave, the child, is man.

סב /62

There is a still earlier version of this lone man sealed in some ancient cave's black hollow. Shielded from the blinding light of the Holy One Himself. Permitted for his own safety to see but a single needle-thin beam of holy light. Until he himself is full of light. So full that it streams from the holes in his face.

". . . an empty vacuum was formed in the midst of the *Ayn Sof* (The Infinite One) into which emanated a ray of light . . . which arranges itself both in concentric circles and in a unilinear structure, which is the form of *Adam Kadmon* . . . the primordial man . . . The *Adam Kadmon* serves as a kind of intermediary link between *Ayn Sof*, the light of whose substance continues to be active in him, and the hierarchy of worlds still to come . . . From the head of the *Adam Kadmon* tremendous lights shone forth and aligned themselves in rich and complex patterns." (Gershom Scholem, *Kabbalah*, Keter Publishing, Jerusalem, 1974, pp. 131,137.)

And as Moses came down from the mountain bearing the two tablets of the pact, Moses was not aware that the skin of his face was radiant. . .

*Exodus
34:29*

‏. . . וּשְׁנֵי לֻחֹת הָעֵדֻת בְּיַד־מֹשֶׁה בְּרִדְתּוֹ מִן־הָהָר וּמֹשֶׁה לֹא־יָדַע כִּי‎
‏קָרַן עוֹר פָּנָיו. . .‎

But no matter how delicate and gentle the Creator beams the light, it is always too much. In one version after another, the bestowing of the light results in some kind of shattering. In the Lurianic version, the vessels that were intended to carry the light of *Adam Kadmon* shattered, their shards scattering and falling, which is reminiscent of the biblical account:

As soon as Moses came near the camp and saw the calf and the dancing, he became enraged, and he hurled the tablets from his hands and shattered them at the foot of the mountain.

*Exodus
32:19*

‏. . . וַיַּשְׁלֵךְ מִיָּדָיו אֶת־הַלֻּחֹת וַיְשַׁבֵּר אֹתָם תַּחַת הָהָר.‎

The light that had been engraved on them was now strewn amidst the rocks at the foot of the mountain.

סג /63

The needle-thin beams of light that penetrate the caves in which we hide from time to time, is the same light that issues from ourselves. Like *Adam Kadmon*, it streams from the openings in our face and in so doing transforms the world around us. The letters of a word. The setting of the sun. The face of a child. It is not in them. Nor is it in us. We are only its vessel. It issues from us and we glide among the objects of creation as a divine being. One divine one passing among other divine ones. Our respective light raising each other from one rung to the next. For light is more than just some opposite-of-darkness condition in which our eyes can see. Light is the medium of consciousness.

"It is consciousness raising itself from the dark oblivion of unconsciousness." (Erich Neumann, *The Origins and History of Consciousness*, Princeton University Press, 1954, p. 6.)

Light is a metaphor for human awareness.
Shining just between matter and energy.
Being between space and time.
Something which is not a thing.
Like fishes in water, we do not know the light is there.
For if every last bit of it were gone
There would be more than darkness.
There would be spiritual oblivion.
If it weren't for You, O Lord, we would be blind.
In Your Light do we see Light.
בְּאוֹרְךָ נִרְאֶה־אוֹר.

*Psalm
36:10*

סד/64

It is no accident that all the great creation tales begin with light. Of all the things that the Creator might have first formed — mountains, waterfalls, stars, flowers,

fruited plains, lions and lambs, leviathans and whirl-
winds, single-celled creatures and man — He made light.
First of all the Holy One fashioned consciousness.

Let us retell the story of this light which is a metaphor
for spiritual awareness:

A light with which the Holy One began the creation. *Let
there be light and there was light.*

*Genesis
1:1*

יְהִי אוֹר וַיְהִי־אוֹר

In the Zohar (the book of spiritual illumination) we read
further of creation. *Some kind of dark flame — blinding
flash — issued forth, from the innermost hiddenness —
from the mystery of the Ayn-Sof, the Infinite One
Himself...*

*Zohar
I
15a*

... בּוֹצִינָא דְּקַרְדִינוּתָא נָפִיק גּוֹ סְתִים דִּסְתִימוּ מֵרָזָא דְּאֵי׳׳ן סוֹ׳׳ף
...

A light that was so dazzling that by it Rabbi Juda, son of
Rabbi Simon, taught that *man could gaze from one end
of the universe to the other.*

*Exodus
Rabba
35:1*

הָאוֹר שֶׁבָּרָא הקב׳׳ה בְּיוֹם רִאשׁוֹן אָדָם צוֹפֶה וּמַבִּיט בּוֹ מִסּוֹף
הָעוֹלָם וְעַד סוֹפוֹ.

A light so powerful that it *shattered earthly vessels.*

*Aytz
Hayim,
Shaar
HaKlalim
ch. 2*

הַכֵּלִים נִשְׁבְּרוּ לְסִבַּת הֱיוֹת הָאוֹר הַגָּדוֹל וְלֹא יָכוֹל לְסוֹבְלוֹ

A light that if it fell into the hands of the wicked could
return creation itself back to primordial chaos. A light

that therefore had to be hidden away. *And God made a separation. . .*

וַיַּבְדֵּל אֱלֹהִים . . .

Genesis 1:4

A light that was set aside for the *Tsadikim*.
Light is sown for the righteous . . .

אוֹר זָרֻעַ לַצַּדִּיק

Psalm 97:11

A light whose appearance initiates creation. But it is a creation only able to withstand a tiny bit of light. Therefore the light had to be concealed. And so it is that darkness and incompletion and separation are the price of this world. While light initiates existence, existence conceals light.

For with the appearance of the light being began,
But with the concealment of the light
*   all manner of individuated existence was created . . .*
Just this is the mystery of the work of creation;
And one who is able to understand will understand.

כִּי בְהוֹפִיעַ הָאוֹר נִתְרָחֵב הָעוֹלָם וּבְגִנְיָזָתוֹ נִבְרְאוּ כָל הַנִּמְצָאִים
לְמִינֵיהֶם . . . כִּי זֶהוּ סוֹד מַעֲשֵׂה בְרֵאשִׁית וְהַמֵּבִין יָבִין

Shimon Lavi, Ketem Paz (Djerba Tunisia, 1940. p.124, col.3)

A light imprisoned in the shards of this created world, waiting for us to free it. Returning itself and us to the Creator.

A light so awesome that even a fraction of its splendor — just so much as a ray the thinness of a needle is all any of us need for unimaginable spiritual illumination.

A light that is shown to each soul before it enters the world and a light that those who have come very close to death and returned, tell of seeing.

A light that flickers at the conclusion of each Shabbos amidst the twisted wicks of the *Havdalla* candle.

A light by which we need fear death no more than the inevitable darkness that begins each night.

A light in which we can reenvision our own ultimate transformation.

In other words, a light by which we experience our creation and our Creator.

And toward which we yearn as does a plant for sunlight, as our ultimate destiny and fulfillment.

You shall further instruct the Israelites to bring you clear oil of beaten olives for light, in order that there should be an eternal light.

Exodus
27:20

... וְיִקְחוּ אֵלֶיךָ שֶׁמֶן זַיִת זָךְ כָּתִית לַמָּאוֹר לְהַעֲלֹת נֵר תָּמִיד

It is as if the One — who is Light —
Left a trace of Himself in His creation at the beginning,
A souvenir, to see if it would grow.

What use is made of oil? It is put into a lamp, and then the two together give light as though they were one.

[100]

Hence, the Holy One will say to Israel, "My children, since my light is your light, and your light is my light, let us go together — you and I — and give light to Zion:" "Arise , give light, for your light has come.

מַה דַּרְכּוֹ שֶׁל שֶׁמֶן לְהִנָּתֵן בַּנֵּר וְהֵן מְאִירִים שְׁנֵיהֶם מֵאַחַת כָּךְ אָמַר הקב״ה לְיִשְׂרָאֵל בָּנַי הוֹאִיל וְאוֹרִי הוּא אוֹרְכֶם וְאוֹרְכֶם הוּא אוֹרִי אֲנִי וְאַתֶּם נֵלֵךְ וְנָאִיר לְצִיּוֹן ״קוּמִי אוֹרִי כִּי בָא אוֹרֵךְ״. . .

Pesikta DeRav Kahana, Kumi Uri 21

Isaiah 60:1

Praised are You O Lord the [only] one who forms Light.

בָּרוּךְ אַתָּה יְיָ יוֹצֵר הַמְּאוֹרוֹת

Daily Prayer-book

סה / 65

The First Light

When one is born he emerges into the light of day. It must surely be dazzling and awesome. So the little one looks around with unfocused eyes and then closes them in order to rest.

Not long ago when our third child, Lev, was born we wanted things to be gentle. There were to be no bright lights or loud noises. No holding him upside down or making him cry. And right after he was born we placed him on Karen's stomach and spoke soft words of joy and welcome, all the while caressing his tiny body. He did not cry at all. And only a few minutes later did he open his eyes. He looked all around and now smiling he closed his eyes.

טז/66

But the light of consciousness with which the world began is yet incomplete. Hidden. Imprisoned. Depending on us. For the Adam-man who left the garden was only partly aware. And, we might say, perhaps only therefore, partly created. Even as we, his children, spend our days in wasted unawareness.

To become aware is to come closer to the Creator. The Holy One. Source of all awareness light. Who is Himself of pure eternal light. To become aware is to join the Holy One in the act of creating oneself.

With a divine prayer were we created,
That the light of awareness should not go out.
Many other worlds were created before this one
But each one of them failed.
Until at last the Creator
Made something a little like Himself:
Light in the shape of a person.

For you see,
We are the result of the desire of awareness,
And the prayer of the Creator,
To comprehend itself.

We are the reification of the inexorable divine urge
To create consciousness.
And thereby fulfill itself.

For consciousness — and You and I — and God —
Live to create more light.

טז /67

In the beginning there was light. The Holy One's urge to create and our eternal yearning to behold creation. But if no one was present at creation, then each of us must know of God's world-making from within ourselves. In which case everyone, including you and me, were there. And are there. To the extent that we are spiritually conscious. Such is the holy mystery of awareness.

Shine it out into space and,
As our visionaries are beginning to understand,
It will ultimately define a perfect circle,
Which will return undiminished to its Creator.
Each one of us at each moment stands between the
    beginning and the end,
At the center of a circle.
In the middle of a sphere of light.
(To the extent that we are aware)
Light is to unawareness what
Holiness is to the profane world.

8

אָדָם קַדְמוֹן

Adam Qadmon

The Body *of the* Universe

וְלֵית לָךְ כָּל שַׁיְיפָא דְקַיְימָא בֵּיהּ בְּבַר נָשׁ
דְּלָא הֲוֵי לָקֳבְלֵיהּ בִּרְיָה בְּעַלְמָא

"There is not a member in the human body that
does not have its counterpart in the created world."

Zohar I 134b

פה /68

The history of humanity might have been the life span of one man. Once there was only one person in the universe: *Adam HaRishon*. And this man had but one commandment: Thou shall not eat of the tree. How simple it all might have been had this Adam-man not had such an uncontrollable hunger for eating knowledge-fruit from the tree. If only he could have held out long enough to satisfy the Creator that our world experiment was a success.

There is a legend (which I once heard from Rabbi Shelly Gordon, may his memory be for a blessing) that concerns itself with just this same possibility. If the first Adam-man had fulfilled the only — and also, therefore, every commandment there was — might we not assume that there would have been no reason to expel him from the garden. No need to populate the world. No need for all the commandments and their transgressions. No need for world history. What if the Creator only intended that there be one person and not teeming billions. And that that one person fulfill only one commandment [cf. Gershom Scholem, *Sabbatai Sevi*, Princeton Univ. Press, 1973, pp. 37-8].

Was not the first Adam-man perhaps created on the eve of the seventh day and given one commandment with the divine hope that he could restrain his unrestrainable hunger for but one span of twenty-four hours? For then the creation venture might have been concluded a prompt success. One man. One commandment. One Sabbath. The first man would have been also the last man. The Adam-man would also have been the Messiah.

Now it is true that this tale enables us to imagine the beginning and the end within one sentence. Within the life span of one person. Whatever it was that happened to mankind happened to the first Adam-man during his one Sabbath-day-long life. One and the same life-force-awareness unites all human history. Couples the beginning with the end.

טס /69

There is a contemporary legend that was first told by Arthur Clarke and visualized by Stanley Kubrick in "20-01" which also tries to unite the beginning and the end. Once, so the tale goes, our planet was visited by some supremely intelligent, beneficient, and curious alien. This visitor noticed that one ape seemed to be fascinated by the moon. All the others were too busy staying alive to have time for such wonderment. The visitor decided to show the moon-watcher how to extend his hand by using a simple tool. And in so doing initiated what has come to be known as human history and, incidently, the visitor's own claim to diety. But since this visiting creator had other galaxies to explore, he devised a clever scheme

whereby he might learn if his experiment would succeed. He planted some kind of cosmic alarm clock on the moon that was set to go off the moment his protégé, the moon-watching man-ape should discover it. For surely if he could rise above his fellow animals enough to reach the moon, then it would be worth the creator's time to return for a reunion.

For all these aeons of humanity, the tale suggests, we have been watched. Our progress and ascent has been hoped for. Somewhere at the furthest reaches of the cosmos there waits someone for some ape-man-child-astronaut-explorer for what will be surely the greatest reunion of them all. Standing there in space the first visitor-creator will welcome the last man-explorer. He will say something like, "So we meet again. I was not sure there for a long time whether you would ever make it. But you have and my experiment has been a success."

Now this tale also, despite its substitution for the ancient Holy One whom religious people call God with some space man (and its obeisance to technology) is also about creation and redemption. Our existence is an experiment.

Our redemption the result of some accomplishment. The end and the beginning are joined by some common purpose. And here too, one and the same life-force awareness unites all human history. Of course here the unity resides in the life of the first visitor-creator/the last visited-redeemer.

Or does it? What if there is as much unity in the countless generations separating the first man-ape and the last man-child-astronaut-explorer as there is in the single seemingly infinite life span of the cosmic visitor? What if all life is really the same life? What if what we call the end of our individual lives is only an illusion? Suppose we, each of us, are as much a part of those who preceed and follow us as our childhood is of our old age? And that like some life disconnected and interrupted by flashes of amnesia, which is, nevertheless the same life, so too with the generations of human history. I cannot remember personally being freed from Egypt but nevertheless I myself was freed from Egypt.

There is another Kabbalistic legend that tells of all humankind descending from another Adam. *Adam Kadmon*, the primordial archetypic man, which the Kabbala is careful to distinguish from *Adam HaRishon*, the first mythic man of the garden, lest the distinction between man and God be confused. But by allowing them both to share the name "Adam" the blasphemous-holy confusion is nevertheless intimated. This primordial Adam was some kind of giant who contained within him the souls of us all. After the Fall they were scattered about the universe like sparks. They are never extinguished. There are only so many of them. They are each an eternal life force that gives life to one creature after another in one generation after another. And each of them began in the same *Adam Kadmon*, the same archetypic man, the same primordial giant. And at the end, they will return once again to their same ancient unity.

Perhaps in some other galaxy it is the way of life to con-

tinue from childhood to adolescence to maturity to old age without interruption or forgetting. Life awareness and continuity might span what we see as generations. But for us of this world, the continuity of life times seem irreparably severed by death and inexplicably initiated by birth. Those life sustaining sparks scattered from *Adam Kadmon* do not seem to be linked from one generation to the next. Somehow our consciousness of our journey is stricken with amnesia.

"Everybody carries the secret trace of the transmigrations of his soul in the lineaments of his forehead and his hands, and in the aura which radiates from his body." (Gershom Scholem, *Major Trends in Jewish Mysticism,* Schocken, 1941, p. 283.)

ע/70

It is said of the holy ones of old that they could look onto a forehead and see to the very depths of a soul. See all its travels and affairs. Transmigrations and incarnations. All its folly and all its holiness. All the way back to its origin on one of the limbs of the first man himself. All the way back to the very root of its existence. All of which grew from one and the same tree.

"Rabbi Simeon ben Lakish said in the name of Rabbi Eleazar ben Azariah: At the time that the Holy One, blessed be He, was creating Adam, He had come to the stage in creating him when Adam had the form of a golem, an unarticulated embryo, *which lay prone from one end of the world to the other. Then the Holy One, blessed be He, caused to pass before the golem each generation with its righteous men, each generation with its wicked men, each generation with its scholars, each generation with its leaders. . ."*

. . . וְהָיָה מוּטָל מִסּוֹף הָעוֹלָם וְעַד סוֹפוֹ. וְהָיָה הַקָּדוֹשׁ בָּרוּךְ הוּא
מַעֲבִיר לְפָנָיו דּוֹר וָדוֹר וְצַדִּיקָיו [דּוֹר וָדוֹר וּרְשָׁעָיו]. . .

Pesikta Rabbati 23:1

And this primordial archetype being is recreated in each embryo, which likewise is permitted to see from one end to the other.

But it is the same thing whether you start at the beginning and understand how Adam foresaw and contained all those yet to issue from him. Or whether you look into your own forehead and follow yourself all the way back to the first man. (Or before and through him to the Holy One Himself.)

עא/71

Like some rare and beautiful insect
Microscopic eggs planted lifetimes ago
Fertilized, nourished, and suspended in time
Waiting for some future moment of just right "accidental" conditions
Pre-ordained to set off some yearning biological alarm clock.

So is the appearance of each and every child.
Waiting for this man and that woman to meet and
Procreate themselves.
The seeds for some rare and beautiful offspring
Planted in them already unaware yet waiting —
By the first man and the first woman.
Even as they carry the seeds of one last one.

עב /72

The first man,
Was more than the first man.
Something of this *Adam HaRishon*
Intimates the last man.
Even as we who are between them
Are something of them both.

As his divine blueprint originally called for,
An Adam also called *Adam Kadmon*,
A being made from pure light
Streaming from the apertures in his face.
Comprehending at once the beginning and the end of
    things.
Smiling the smile only mimicked by the great religious
    teachers of old.
At one with the universe.
This is the primordial Adam, *Adam Kadmon*

Perhaps also to be confused with the *Atika Kadisha*, the Holy Ancient One Himself.

Rabbi Simeon ben Lakish said, in the order of things created on the last day, Adam came last, but in the order of the whole creation, he came first. Such was the opinion of Resh Lakish, as Resh Lakish pointed out on the verse, "The spirit of God hovered over the face of the waters." The spirit of God referring to Adam's spirit.

(Genesis 1:2)

"אָמַר שִׁמְעוֹן בֶּן לָקִישׁ אָחוֹר לְמַעֲשֶׂה יוֹם אַחֲרוֹן וְקֶדֶם לְמַעֲשֶׂה בְרֵאשִׁית זֶה דַּעְתֵּיהּ דְּרֵישׁ לָקִישׁ דְּאָמַר רֵישׁ לָקִישׁ וְרוּחַ אֱלֹהִים מְרַחֶפֶת עַל־פְּנֵי הַמַּיִם זֶה רוּחוֹ שֶׁל אָדָם הָרִאשׁוֹן"

Midrash Tehillim 139.5

... And the spirit of God likewise also is the last man:

וְרוּחַ אֱלֹהִים מְרַחֶפֶת זֶה רוּחוֹ שֶׁל מֶלֶךְ מָשִׁיחַ

Genesis Rabba 2.4

And just this is the idea:
That within each of us is
The blueprint for the universe.
We are of it.
It is of us.
And that the universe from the beginning to the end of
    time
Is, the body of the Holy Ancient One.

As the *Adam Kadmon* was a constellation of all soul
    seeds to come,
And as each cell carries sealed within it the genotype of
    itself,
So each of us is the whole universe.
Notions of big and small are only irrelevant and confus-
    ing here.

[113]

For as we have known all along
(After all it is foretold in our very bones)
The astrophysicist and the biochemist are studying
The very same thing.

In this way we understand that the history of each
    person
And therefore the history of all humanity
And of probably the universe itself (whatever that is)
Is the same.

If no person were present at creation
Then we must know of the story of the beginning
From within ourselves.

People seem to know intuitively what is going on within
their own bodies without medical corroboration. They
understand when they are dying and when they are getting well. Perhaps their bodies also "feel" the forces
working for the unification of the universe itself.

We read in the Zohar:
*There is not a member in the human body that does not
have its counterpart in the created world. For as a
person's body may be divided into members and organs,
each performing a hierarchy of functions, each acting
and reacting upon one another so as to form one
organism, so it is also with the entire world. Each one of
its created parts are likewise members meant to exist in a
hierarchy and when properly arranged one with the
other form one organic body.*

The body of the universe.

Zohar
I
134b

וְלֵית לָךְ כָּל שַׁיְיפָא וְשַׁיְיפָא דְקַיְימָא בֵיה בְּבַר נָשׁ דְּלָא הֲוֵי
לָקָבְלֵיה בִּרְיָה בְּעַלְמָא דְּהָא כְּמָה דְּבַר נָשׁ אִיהוּ מִתְפְּלִיג שַׁיְיפִין
וְכֻלְהוּ קַיְימִין דַּרְגִּין עַל דַּרְגִּין מִתְתַּקְנִין אִלֵּין עַל אִלֵּין וְכֻלְהוּ חַד
גוּפָא הָכִי נָמֵי עַלְמָא כָל אִינּוּן בִּרְיָין כֻּלְהוּ שַׁיְיפִין שַׁיְיפִין וְקַיְימִין
אִלֵּין עַל אִלֵּין וְכַד מִתְתַּקְנָן כֻּלְהוּ הָא חַד גוּפָא מַמָּשׁ

עג/73

In other words the body of the universe and the human archetype are identical. You might ask, how could the universe have a body? In only the same way that you and I can have an archetype.

If light is awareness, then creation stories, beginning with light, are man telling about himself. Ink blots of some long ago present. Mirrors in which we might see back through the adolescent sophistication of which we are so proud.

Once we tried to pluck out our eyes in a vain attempt at objectivity. Then we learned that some subjectivity is inescapable. As Heisenberg discovered: to observe is to participate. We change what we look at simply by looking at it. So we left our eyes in our heads. Now we are being coaxed to look at one's eyes themselves. For the thinker is thinking about himself.

Our drive to find the light hidden long ago can only lead us back to an awareness of ourselves.

"I have been taught by my teacher that something of the first man resembled that first light which was concealed (leaving only) afterwards a thread-thin ray ... know this: It is one secret and one foundation and I am unable to expound upon this any further. For thus I have been commanded ..."

Ketem
Paz,
ibid.
121,
col. 2

וְהוֹרֵנִי מְלַמְּדִי כִּי הָיָה עִנְיָנוֹ שֶׁל אָדָם הָרִאשׁוֹן כִּדְמְיוֹן הָאוֹר הָרִאשׁוֹן שֶׁנִּגְנַז וְאַחַר כָּךְ הוֹפִיעַ חוּט מִמֶּנוּ ... וְהָבֵן זֶה כִּי הַסּוֹד אֶחָד הוּא וִיסוֹד אֶחָד וְלֹא אוּכַל לְהַרְחִיב בּוֹ כִּי כֵן צֻוֵּיתִי

We are, in other words, part of what we seek to study. Perhaps all of what we seek to study. The mystery is trying to become aware of itself. The one who is the riddle is trying to solve the riddle. Ultimate awareness can surely be no more than ultimate personal awareness. Even as ultimate awareness can only bring us together with the cosmos.

עד /74

To the extent that we are conscious
We become the largest and most distant
And the smallest and most intimate non-stuff there is.
In other words,
To be aware, to be conscious
Is perhaps to liken ourselves with the farthest and the
nearest
With the earliest — and we must assume the last.

עה /75

There are two directions of astonishment. Here is how it happens. Above there arches the immensity of the heavens. That if the thickness of this page of paper were to equal the 93 million miles between the earth and the sun then the distance to the edge of the known universe would be a stack of papers 31 million miles high.

And within there breathes the intricacy of the human body. That in each of the 100 trillion cells there are roughly 100,000 genes coiled on a molecule of deoxyribonucleic acid which if uncoiled and unwound would string back and forth between the earth and the sun over 400 times.

Man stands at the center of these two infinite directions. Above him space and time are literally astronomic. Within him space and time are infinitesimal. And now we understand that the universe is expanding. Growing ever larger. And that with each new microscope the inner biology grows ever smaller. In a word: we will never see the farthest thing above nor the smallest thing within. The greatness of the distance and the minuteness of the size will always increase simultaneously. It is almost as if we were driven to maintain this balance that always leaves us in the center.

Astrophysicists now posit a universe that is constantly expanding. Molecular biologists are less willing to iden-

tify some ultimate indivisible particle. Unless, of course, both would cautiously settle on light in its fastest (time-space-matter-energy) form or light in its smallest (a particle that no longer has the properties of a particle-photon-wave) form.

Beyond the farthest reaches. Within the innermost depths. Light sparkles. Consciousness shines. Awareness permeates the universe.

". . . As we keep on investigating matter, we will work down from crystals to molecules, from molecules to atoms, from atoms to particles, from particles to quarks — and mine to forever greater depths . . . The analysis of the physical world, pursued to sufficient depth, will lead back in some now-hidden way to man himself, to conscious mind, tied unexpectedly through the very acts of observation and participation to partnership in the foundation of the universe." (John Archibald Wheeler, "The Universe as Home for Man" in *American Scientist* 62, Nov./Dec. 1974, p. 689.)

עו /76

In the biology of the cell
The boundary between life and non-life blurs.
Less "things" are just things than they used to be.
And at the bottom of it all
There will probably be
"Things" more like energy than matter.

More like time than space.
Just as matter becomes energy,
and just as space becomes time,
Light is formed.
Myriads of tiny photons of whirring light.
Light which is but a metaphor for human awareness.
Awareness, which is but another name
For the ultimate evolutionary expression of man.
At last reunited with his Creator.
In the primordial and messianic light of consciousness.

עז /77

Adam HaRishon, the first man and the last man are one and the same. The one who left the garden in order to continue eating from knowledge will, after all the generations have come and gone, at long last be sated. **Even as he will be the same one who will be called God's anointed one. The Messiah who will return to the garden.**

If we had remained in Eden we would have been as one with the universe. But we never could have been conscious of our unity. So we left seeking that unity and consciousness. Leaving the garden is a metaphor for our forgetting that we are one with the universe. Holy awareness is the only way to return.

And by drawing this primordial man
Who is also us,

We draw the universe.
And by envisioning the heavens
We portray our own
Human consciousness.

סְפִירוֹת

Sefirot

Higher Worlds

קָדְשָׁא בְּרִיךְ הוּא אַפִּיק עֲשֶׂר כִּתְרִין עִטְרִין קַדִּישִׁין
לְעֵילָה דְּאִתְעַטָּר בְּהוּ וּמִתְלַבַּשׁ בְּהוּ וְהוּא אִינוּן
וְאִינוּן הוּא כְּשַׁלְהוֹבָא דַּאֲחִידָא בְּגוּמְרָא

"The Holy One blessed be He offers ten holy
crowns on high with which He adorns Himself and
clothes Himself. And He is they; and they are He,
like a flame is joined to a burning coal."

Zohar III 70a

עת /78

There are higher holier worlds than this one.
Obviously no one can know how many there are.
Nor can we be certain
That a certain rung of holy awareness
   Is the same for differnt persons.
We only know that most of the time,
We are busy here,
Below the bottom one.
And that above the top one is the Nameless One,
The one named *Ayn Sof*, the One without end.
And that He comes down to us, as it were,
Like light poured down
Through some cascading waterfall.
And that we go up to Him
Through the same network,
Like salmon returning upstream to spawn.
But that whether like water down a fall
Or creatures swimming home,
By the time each reaches its destination
There is not much remaining.
Only a thin diluted version of what once started out.
So that what we see of Him here
Is dim.
And what He sees of us on high,
While very true to what we really are,
Might not look the way we do
To each other.

But in any case, ordinary souls like you and I are the link between this world and the higher ones, shuttling back and forth, carrying buckets of light in our heads.

עט /79

Now these channels
Through which God and man commute to each other
Are understood by many analogies.
Each of them are but one
Of the infinite number of ways
Of representing the meeting
With the Holy One.
The ascent of souls.
And yet each is accurate:

In the heavens above there are palaces or *hechalot:* Lush meadows, chambers like valleys, awaiting the traveler. Each room brighter than the one before.

Each person is a unique replica of the primordial human *Adam Kadmon.* And this archetype is also the body of the universe. A manifestation of consciousness in the shape of a person. ". . . with light streaming from the apertures in his face. . ."

The creation of the world is a metaphor for the emergence of awareness. So that returning to our genesis, be it cosmic to the furthest reaches of the heavens or microscopic to sub-atomic particles, leads likewise through concentric spheres of increasing/decreasing size. There are ten modes of awareness.

Human consciousness, inner spiritual space, can likewise be set in a diagram. The map will suggest the paradox of encountered reality and the balance within the human soul. It must therefore also have an axis of symmetry. A right side and a left side. Masculine and feminine. It will intimate that there are ever increasing spheres above and ever diminishing spheres within. It will be in the shape of a person. Or it will be like a family tree that can either suggest how one's progenitors conspired to make one man or how one person conspired to populate the universe. In other words a tree on which you place yourself as the seed of the root or the bud on the uppermost branch.

The drawing might also be envisioned as the process whereby the Holy One created man. Or whereby souls reach towards an awareness of their Creator. And thus the image will suggest how we and God are connected through a network of channels. Drawn to one another through their mutual need to reunite. The expression of which we understand to be the Torah.

Proverbs 3:18   *Behold it is a tree of life . . .* עֵץ חַיִּים הִיא

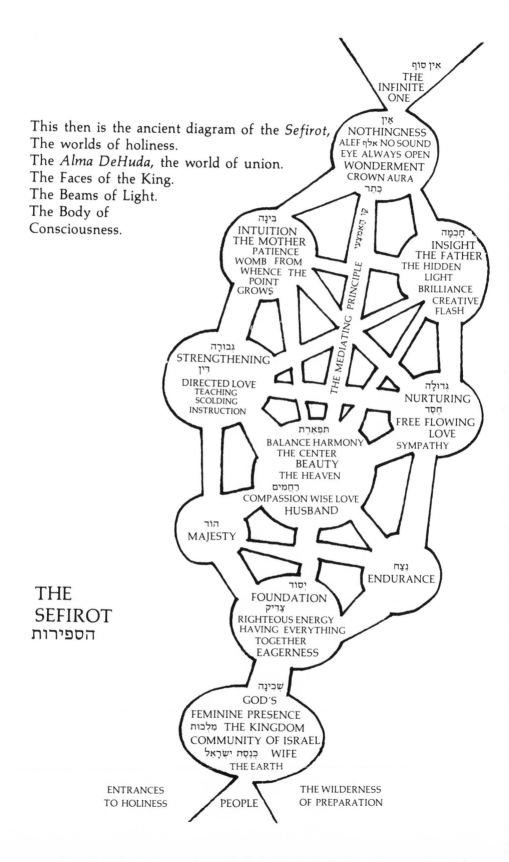

This then is the ancient diagram of the *Sefirot*,
The worlds of holiness.
The *Alma DeHuda,* the world of union.
The Faces of the King.
The Beams of Light.
The Body of
Consciousness.

אֵין סוֹף
THE INFINITE ONE

אַיִן
NOTHINGNESS
אלף ALEF NO SOUND
EYE ALWAYS OPEN
WONDERMENT
CROWN AURA
כֶּתֶר

בִּינָה
INTUITION
THE MOTHER
PATIENCE
WOMB FROM
WHENCE THE
POINT
GROWS

חָכְמָה
INSIGHT
THE FATHER
THE HIDDEN
LIGHT
BRILLIANCE
CREATIVE
FLASH

קַו הַאֶמְצָעִי
THE MEDIATING PRINCIPLE

גְבוּרָה
STRENGTHENING
דִין
DIRECTED LOVE
TEACHING
SCOLDING
INSTRUCTION

גְדוּלָה
NURTURING
חֶסֶד
FREE FLOWING
LOVE
SYMPATHY

תִפְאֶרֶת
BALANCE HARMONY
THE CENTER
BEAUTY
THE HEAVEN
רַחֲמִים
COMPASSION WISE LOVE
HUSBAND

הוֹד
MAJESTY

נֶצַח
ENDURANCE

יְסוֹד
FOUNDATION
צַדִיק
RIGHTEOUS ENERGY
HAVING EVERYTHING
TOGETHER
EAGERNESS

THE
SEFIROT
הספירות

שְׁכִינָה
GOD'S
FEMININE PRESENCE
מַלְכוּת THE KINGDOM
COMMUNITY OF ISRAEL
כְּנֶסֶת יִשְׂרָאֵל WIFE
THE EARTH

ENTRANCES
TO HOLINESS

PEOPLE

THE WILDERNESS
OF PREPARATION

פ /80

This world.
The one in which you are reading these words
Is at the center of concentric worlds.
They are each bigger than this place.
They are higher.
Holier and more real than this world.

Shabbos is more real than Wednesday.
Jerusalem is more real than Chicago.
The *sukka* is more real than a garage.
Tsadakkah is more real than income tax.
Holy is more real than profane.
Standing closer to the Holy One is more real than being
    far from Him.

But they are also smaller than this ordinary world.
For they are within it.

There are many degrees of holiness. Perhaps as described
by the school of Luria: Doing, Formation, Creation, and
Emanation. Or perhaps as we read elsewhere, "The
world was created with ten words". There are ten
Sefirot, or spheres, or words. Or 310 worlds, *Shai
Olamot*, hinted at in the final mishna of Tractate Uktsin
or the 390 of Tractate Derekh Eretz Rabba (ch. 2).

Spiritual journeys can only be chronicled but not reported. What we speak of once we have returned are like stories from our childhood or legends from of old.

While you can speak of higher worlds from within lower ones with seeming accuracy, you can really only comprehend a higher world from within it.

פא/81

We are mistaken to imagine that we can share the understanding of higher worlds with those who have remained behind. This is because the awareness of holier worlds shatters earthenware vessels unable to withstand the light. To try to speak of the Holy One in the language of this world is already to speak of something else other than the Holy One.

Each world has a logic unique to it. In this world for instance, the logic of Aristotle dominates. Nothing can be its opposite.

When we try to speak of what we have learned from a higher world, the logic from that place we bring down with us betrays us and we sound illogical. For instance, while it is true that this world is at the center and higher ones encircle out from it, it is also true that the highest world is the center and that this world is on the outermost periphery.

A pinpoint of light in the very center of a perfectly still mirror-smooth and formless black ocean. And from that creative and divine interruption there rippled an infinite number of concentric circles of increasing diameter but diminishing light.

The levels of ascent might be represented alternatively as:

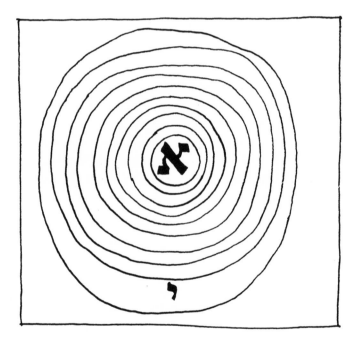

With the Infinite One being at the center of introspection.

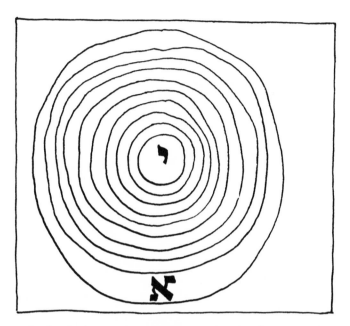

Or with the Infinite One being at the farthest reaches of the cosmos. But they are both the same. Even as the diagrams of the ten *Sefirot* and the form of *Adam Kadmon*, the primordial man, are but different ways of representing the same thing. All manifestations of the Holy King.

פב /82

This is the way you will go to higher worlds. You will pay great attention to the most trivial matters. Their great subtlety makes them elusive to most people who

are too anxious to get on with things. Allow yourself to dwell as if forever on the very first thought, for instance. The one you quickly gloss over since it is surely impossible, lascivious, preposterous or silly. Yes. That is the one. To dwell — even for a moment — on the tiniest, most unlikely thought is the beginning.

It is as if there were gateways. And at each one there stands a guard who wants nothing from you. Except that you go away. He will do all in his great power to foil your ascent. But his power is only the evil within you.

"When the world was created God first made the trees. And then afterwards He made iron. The trees shook with terror as they foresaw now the making of axes and their eventual demise. Said God. Don't be afraid. If you give none of your wood, there can be no handles with which to make axes."

Genesis Rabba 5:9

‏... כֵּיוָן שֶׁנִּבְרָא הַבַּרְזֶל הִתְחִילוּ הָאִילָנוֹת מְרַתְּתִים, אָמַר לָהֶם מַה לָכֶם מְרַתְּתִים עֵץ מִכֶּם אַל יִכָּנֵס בִּי וְאֵין אֶחָד מִכֶּם נִזּוֹק.

The guard of one of the gates is the notion you have that trivial matters are trivial. That little things are unimportant. Or that for example, the first thought, the one you quickly gloss over is silly. He is very good at his job, this guard of the first gate, is he not?

Then no sooner is he passed by than you will meet another guard. Boredom. Turn to counting things.

Daydream. Watch television. Sleep. Eat. Things that another time might themselves be entrances themselves, in the hands of the second guard, are great barriers.

And Jacob dreamt and there was a ladder and — get this— messengers were going *up* and *down* on it. It does not say *down* and *up*. But up and down. The messengers begin on earth and return to earth. Perhaps, as one legend has it, they are princes of all the nations and Jacob is you and I who hears God coaxing, Please come up. If you come up all the way history will end. No one will have dominion over you any longer. But Jacob — like you and I — is afraid. And remains earthbound. *The Holy One said to him, "Don't be afraid. If you come up you will never have to go back down to the mundane world." But he didn't believe Him. And so he didn't go up.*

אָמַר לוֹ הַקָּדוֹשׁ בָּרוּךְ הוּא: וְאַתָּה אַל תִּירָא אִם אַתָּה עוֹלֶה אֵין
לְךָ יְרִידָה עוֹלָמִית לֹא הֶאֱמִין וְלֹא עָלָה

Leviticus Rabba 29.2

Such fear is probably another gate keeper. There it is before us and we panic at the last minute unable to climb another step higher. We say to ourselves that we are being wise or cautious but we know we are lying. And Jacob awoke the next morning and realized that it had not been a dream and that he had indeed spent the night at the gateway to heaven. And he was angry with himself and built a little shrine there. A marker to his cowardice.

פג /83

*The story of an accidental (?) encounter
between one coming down and one going out
who were surprised to meet*

We have a front porch. When I was a boy such a thing was called a stoop. During the summer, since we don't want to afford air conditioning, we just leave the front door open all the time. So there is only the screen door banging shut from the kids running in and out, letting all the bugs in.

But before I go on, there is something else. Have you ever tried to get close to a bird? Sure you did. When you were little. But they always flew away. The children of humanity simply cannot get close to wild birds. Oh, sometimes you can sneak up on a pigeon in the park. But somehow you feel like its not the real pigeon you're getting close to. Just some facade the pigeon sets up in order not to frighten you and get on with the popcorn. I think it's that way with these household canaries, too.

Well, I had to get out of the house. There was too much commotion. Sometimes it is that way even with the people you love the most. So I pushed open the screen door and got one foot out onto the stoop.

In another universe something else happened. There was a bird that was being very careless. I suspect that it was too busy fleeing for its bird-life to worry about very much else. She was (I am not sure she was a she) flying down from a tree, exhausted. Looking for a place to alight.

And for a moment which was too long for each of us we both stood on the same stoop. Silently saying to one another, you're not supposed to be here. Oh yeah, well neither are you. We two do not belong in this place at the same time. So the bird flew back up to another tree. And I went inside. Even for a moment it had lasted long enough. Souls from different worlds rarely choose to meet one one another voluntarily.

"You speak to us," they said to Moses, "and we will listen, but don't let God speak to us, lest we die."

וַיֹּאמֶר אֶל־מֹשֶׁה דַּבֶּר־אַתָּה עִמָּנוּ וְנִשְׁמָעָה וְאַל־יְדַבֵּר עִמָּנוּ אֱלֹהִים פֶּן־נָמוּת

Exodus 20:16

פד /84

When we stood at the foot of Sinai and God asked if we wanted His Torah, we replied all at once, *We will do and we will hear!*

וַיֹּאמְרוּ כֹּל אֲשֶׁר־דִּבֶּר יְהֹוָה נַעֲשֶׂה וְנִשְׁמָע

Exodus 24:7

In those days we understood enough to know that doing in this world must precede receiving holy awareness. This is because the way to such understanding is by do-

ing. And doing is the only thing that can be done here in the wilderness.

And such indeed is the definitive mark of any would-be Jewish spirituality. That the way to God comes only through religious doing. And that religious doing can only occur in this world. And for this reason this world is holy, too. For some searchers it is a necessary evil, something to cast off. For us it is the only way of ascending to other worlds. It is not a stumbling block or obstacle that must be avoided. It is the very way itself. It is not our way, our goal as the children of Jacob, to leave this world of broken vessels and misplaced love. But rather to go out to it.

The path to holiness is only profane if it is seen as a means to an end. But for us, the end is only as holy as the least holy of the several means we employ. We begin with whatever is set before us. Doing — not to it — but with it, in accordance with His will.

In other words, you must do in the place where you are, the only thing that can be done in that place, for that is the only way to get to the next place. If you try only to attain spiritual understanding here you will get nothing done and understand nothing. But if you try to do holy deeds here you will get a little bit done and so rise to higher worlds. Worlds where the only thing you can do is understand. And once you understand, you will be able to return to this place with enough understanding to do what is next to be done.

פה/85

Organized religion is our attempt to keep visions of other worlds present in this one. And this is why the religious endeavor tangles us in self-contradiction. For to speak of the other world in the language of this world is impossible.

Judaism focuses on the point where the two worlds meet: Sinai. And the inscrutable record of that encounter: Torah. We seem to gain our invitation to the holy world by virtue of our presence there at that awesome mountain. Because the Jew is a member of a community who was present when the other world flooded this one with meaning, we are able to return as often as we wish, simply by remembering.

פו/86

At the center of any great religious movement — be it historical or personal — are encounters with the Holy One. So awesome and life-changing is their force, that to remember them without word or act would constitute a denial of life. Such is the origin of ritual and story. They give witness through sacred act and holy word to some meeting with the Nameless One. But to our great frustration, in the process of transmitting the kernel, the mo-

ments they would recall become encrusted. Ossified through centuries of unquestioning repetition. But the kernel remains within them for any who are daring and desirous enough. A spiritual fire: Sacred ritual and holy story are none other than the detritus of the lost encounter between man and the Holy One. A record of a meeting that has taken place. Is taking place. Will continue to take place. As long as souls yearn.

You must disregard all explanations. For all explanations by definition must follow the searing reality of the event itself. They are composed by people who were not wise enough to appreciate the existential significance of the encounter, or too afraid to tell the story in the first person.

פז /87

There is no way to convince someone that you have been to a higher world. For nothing can be brought down save the memories of a dream.

One by one we encounter the unnamed and unnameable
   Holiness.
And because we would bring it back with us
To remind ourselves and share with others and,
   perhaps even boast a little,
We ask of the Nameless One: What is your name?
(Would you mind standing over there in the sunlight
   for just a moment so I can get a good snapshot?)
But He never tells us.

Jacob asked, "Please tell me your name." But He said,
"You must not ask my name . . ."

וַיִּשְׁאַל יַעֲקֹב וַיֹּאמֶר הַגִּידָה־נָּא שְׁמֶךָ וַיֹּאמֶר לָמָּה זֶּה תִּשְׁאַל לִשְׁמִי

Genesis
32:30

When the Holy One revealed Himself to Moses at the
bush, "Moses said to God, 'When I come to the Israelites
and say to them, 'The God of your fathers has sent me to
you,' and they ask me, "What is His name?" "What
shall I say to them?" And God said to Moses. "I will be
whatever I will be."

וְאָמְרוּ־לִי מַה־שְּׁמוֹ מָה אֹמַר אֲלֵהֶם וַיֹּאמֶר אֱלֹהִים אֶל־מֹשֶׁה
אֶהְיֶה אֲשֶׁר אֶהְיֶה

Exodus
3:13,14

Moses realized, at the last minute, that he would need
some sign, some bit of convincing evidence, that he had
indeed met the Most High and was doing His bidding.
But God said what He always says, "I'm sorry but I can't
help you; I'll be whatever I'll be. Alive and real. And
therefore unpredictable. Look Moses, don't you know by
now that they won't believe you anyway. Whatever trick
I show you the Egyptian magicians will be able to
match."

In such matters there is no compelling evidence. You
cannot transport the wisdom of such a holy awareness as
this moment into every-day slave reality.

"You and I, Moses will have to trick them into leaving
the slave pits of Egypt — for we can never get them to
believe either one of us as long as they are there."

God, He is very wise.
He knows that once we learn His name

[137]

(And remember that there are seventy-two mystical
    names of God — all of which are incorrect anyway.)
He can no longer be God.
Or to put it another way,
The moment you learn a new name for God,
It can no longer be a name for God.
For the Nameless One can have no name
That we can know.

פח /88

And Jacob had a dream
And right there in that God forsaken place
There was a channel
Standing on the earth.
Yet reaching to the very heavens.
And holy messengers were going up
    And going down on it.

Sometimes. The channel is not apparent.
The upper worlds and the lower worlds
Seem hopelessly isolated from one another.
And then in a moment,
In some very unlikely place,
A ladder appears where before there was only the void.
And those who were below may ascend;
And those who were above may come down to earth.
As if some great channel lock were opened.
And radiance like honey flows down from on high.

פט /89

The Loving Star

Since Levy's birth, six months ago, everyone's position in the family has obviously undergone profound change. We have all had to do some adjusting as a new soul began to take his place in our family system. The children especially were worried whether or not there would still be enough love to go around and took to quarrelling even more than usual. And then I came up with this idea.

On a piece of paper with everyone watching on, I drew a figure that looked something like this:

There was much excitement. "Daddy, what is it?" But, I just went on drawing. Then in each circle I wrote the name of one of our family. Then I drew arrows, pointed in both directions extending between each person and everyone else in the family. I explained to everyone that the arrows were lines of loving and that the more love someone "put out" into the system—since every channel flowed in two directions but also sooner or later lead back to itself — the more one "got back." I wrote at the top, "The loving always comes back to you" and at the bottom, "You can't take loving, you can only give loving." And I titled it, "The Kushner Family Loving Star." We taped it to the wall at a young one's eye level.

Every now and then I notice that one of the children is quietly studying the star. They trace the lines with their finger. Somehow drawing some reassurance from the drawing's truth.

Is that not the great childhood problem — and therefore the great human problem: To learn that it is good for you when other people love other people besides you. That I have a stake in their love. That I get more when others give to others.

That if I hoard it,
I loose it.
That if I give it away,
I get it back.

In Henry Miller's words:
"Not to possess power but to radiate it."
(Sunday After the War, N. Y New Directions, pp. 154-5.)

Perhaps it is not accidental that the ancient Kabbalistic diagrams that chart the worlds of holier reality above and within, portray the flow of being as capable of moving in both directions. Perhaps there is an organic innerconnectedness between each world. A kind of inevitable homeostatic balance.

In much the same way as in the human body/psyche.
We read in the morning prayers
"Blessed are You Lord our God, King of the Universe,
Who has formed people in wisdom.
Who created in each of us a life system of organs and
   openings.
And when we are before Your Throne we know
That were one closed that should be open or
That were one open that should be closed,
Life could no longer go on.
And we would no longer be able to stand in Your
   presence.
Blessed are You Lord who heals us with miracles."

Daily
Prayer-
book

... אֲשֶׁר יָצַר אֶת־הָאָדָם בְּחָכְמָה וּבָרָא בוֹ נְקָבִים נְקָבִים חֲלוּלִים

חֲלוּלִים ... בָּרוּךְ אַתָּה יְיָ רוֹפֵא כָל בָּשָׂר וּמַפְלִיא לַעֲשׂוֹת

This overflowing radiance
These emanations
This holy light
Streams down from on High
Fills us and raises us up
And we reciprocate by permitting
The same holy light within us
To travel upward
And holy messengers were going up and down on it.

Genesis
28:12

וְהִנֵּה מַלְאֲכֵי אֱלֹהִים עֹלִים וְיֹרְדִים בוֹ

One of the kids wanted to know where God was on the
"Kushner Family Loving Star" and after talking about it
for a while we wrote the Hebrew letter *Hay* —
representing "His Name" in the very center of the star.

יִחוּד

Yichud

The Eternal One

שְׁמַע יִשְׂרָאֵל יְהוָֹה אֱלֹהֵינוּ יְהוָֹה אֶחָד

"Hear Israel. The Lord our God. The Lord is One."

Deuteronomy 6:4

צ /90

And the last secret is that everything is One.

The beginning was seeing for even one moment
That there was something more to reality
Than meets the eye.
The end is seeing for even one moment
That the apparent multiplicity
Is in reality a unity.

That this moment is all there is.
That this everything is one and therefore nothing.
That something came from nothing
And that at this moment everything will
Return to nothing.

That coursing through the veins of the
Universe at this moment is a kind of
Light in which man and the Holy One are
Yearning to be one.

Deuter- Hear O' Israel, the Lord our God, the Lord is One.
onomy
6:4 שְׁמַע יִשְׂרָאֵל יְהֹוָה אֱלֹהֵינוּ יְהֹוָה אֶחָד

At night when you lie down,
In the morning when you get up,
When you go for a walk,
When you stay home,
The whisper is always the same —
"The Lord is One."

Both opposing sides merge forming one One.
And that that very yearning
And that that simple awareness
Will make them One.
The Lord will be One and His Name One.
... יִהְיֶה יְהֹוָה אֶחָד וּשְׁמוֹ אֶחָד

Zechariah
14:9

צא /91

Could not several people be members of a single living
organic unity. If one person can in sickness or sin be
fragmented, cannot several people in holiness be one?

Where does a person end and begin? Is it really at the
outer border of one's skin? As if to say everything that is
inside is person, everything outside, non-person. Is this
not saying that our least subtle sense, the sense of touch,
defines a person? And what if our ability to see were as
fine as that of the electron microscope? When we came to
the skin line there would still be spaces. Or if we were, as
we probably are, able to see infra-red energy patterns, a
person's shape would so change again. Or what of the
influence a person has? Does a respected person's
boundary end with his or her outer skin?

Where does anything begin and another thing end? If all
the cells in a body are replaced many times during a
single lifetime, then what makes a person the "same"
person? Why have we so ruthlessly superimposed
borders on things? Fragmented the cosmos. Maybe there

are no "objects." Maybe we have only invented them! Agreed to pretend they are, so we can exploit, use and control. Hoping thereby somehow to outwit death. But we do not realize that the very means we have chosen to stay alive fragment us from ourselves and from one another and from our source of life and therefore are what kills us in the end.

The fragmenting, controlling, separating, saying that one thing ends here and another begins there. I own this. Control that. Extend my boundaries to there. Over yours. Will have more. Be more. Live longer. But surely this is death. Suppose instead that we are all of one piece.

צב /92

The Goblet

Seven families with three times as many children are all in a friend's recreation room. We have arranged long tables surrounded by chairs for everyone. In addition to candles and loaves of halla, each family has brought seven times part of the meal. The room is so crowded that only the people near the stairs to the kitchen can bring down the food. The children of course can—and do — come and go by crawling under and over the tables. But the rest of us are committed to our places. We are going to have a communal Sabbath meal.

There is lighting candles. *Kiddush* — the sanctification of the wine and the day. Parents blessing children. Hus-

bands and wives seeing each other with their cautious erotic remembering and yearning. The blessing over the bread. And the food. And more food. With such food, Napoleon's armies could have withstood the Russian winter. Why do Jews always bring so much food!?

And the laughing. The sharing. And the singing. One melody is scarcely spent when another comes forward. We don't even notice the racket of the children. There is a great holiness in this room. It grows from the sharing.

Now we have this *Kiddush* cup which is a large ceramic goblet. It was made for us when we lived in Chicago. I refill it and offer it to Karen. Then to the sculptor, who to my surprise, does not return it. Instead he hands it to his wife with the solemn instructions, "Here, keep it going." And we do. From hand to hand. Drunk from and refilled. Time and time again.

צג /93

We read that *one who saves a single life within humanity is as if they had saved all humanity.*

כָּל־הַמְקַיֵּים נֶפֶשׁ אַחַת מִבְּנֵי אָדָם מַעֲלֶה עָלָיו הַכָּתוּב כְּאִילוּ קִיֵּים עוֹלָם מָלֵא

Sanhedrin 4.5

How is it possible for one soul to save the world?
This is because one soul can be the whole world.
The universe within a soul is more than just an analogue
   to the universe without.

[147]

For one person to make full and complete
Teshuva/repentance/turning/returning and
Return all the way to their source/their Creator,
It is told: Will the entire universe be forgiven

גְּדוֹלָה תְּשׁוּבָה שֶׁבִּשְׁבִיל יָחִיד שֶׁעָשָׂה תְּשׁוּבָה מוֹחֲלִין לְכָל הָעוֹלָם
כֻּלּוֹ

Returning here to one's source means to unify
The inner world and the outer world.
That is, to tell the truth about yourself,
    to yourself and to others
And since there is more than a literary parallel between
    yourself and the universe,
Then if you make one that which is within and without
    yourself,
You would also make one an external apparent senseless
    world with its higher holy source.
That somehow one soul can bring together
Upper worlds with this world.

There are such moments of unification in the lives
    of each individual.
They stand holding this world in one hand
    and the upper worlds in the other.
And by simply being in-between the two
    for even a second,
They are one.
The soul is one.
The worlds are One.

Hear O' Israel the Lord your God
The One you serve

[148]

THE ETERNAL ONE

Wants more than anything
To be one
With you
And Himself
The wandering exiled dove.
If I could only keep the unity before me
For more than a second
The worlds would be unified
But I am distracted by the television
And am broken.
The ideal is probably to take the television commercial
   with me
Into the unity.
But such strength is almost inconceivable.

All that is necessary to unify the worlds
Is to be aware that it is only by an illusion
That they seem to be separate at all.

Or: This world is broken and fragmented
Because not even one soul can remain aware
That the brokenness of this place is a mere illusion
For more than a second.

If you or I could but go on seeing through the illusion
To the great holy stream of light
That binds everything to each other
And their common source
In one great holy Yichud/unity
It would kindle a fire never to be extinguished.

Every now and then one emerges
Who is somehow able to pierce the illusion

And unite the worlds.
Such a man was Abraham, our father, *Avraham Avinu*,
The friend of God.

We read in *Tanhuma* that Rabbi Shimon said about the
verse, *"And they heard the voice of God* [not 'walking
in', as it is customarily rendered but] *leaving the garden
(of Eden)"*

*Genesis
3:8*

וַיִּשְׁמְעוּ אֶת־קוֹל יְהוָֹה אֱלֹהִים מִתְהַלֵּךְ בַּגָּן

Adam came and sinned and God's Presence left the earth
for the heavens.

Cain arose and killed his brother and she went from the
first heaven to the second.

Came the generation of Enosh and spited God further
and she went from the second to the third.

Came the generation of the flood with its perversity and
she went from the third to the fourth.

Came the generation of the separation (of tongues at
Babel) with its arrogance and drove her from the
fourth to the fifth.

Then the Sodomites polluted themselves and drove her
from the fifth to the sixth.

And then there arose Amraphael [the idolatrous king]
and his company and drove her from the sixth
to the seventh and most distant heaven.

*Until Abraham who (at last) was a righteous one arose
And drew God's Presence from the seventh down to the
sixth . . .*

*Tanhuma
Pekuday
6*

. . . עָמַד אַבְרָהָם וְסִגֵּל מַעֲשִׂים טוֹבִים נִמְשְׁכָה הַשְּׁכִינָה מִן שְׁבִיעִי
לַשִּׁשִּׁי

And this is why we read elsewhere:

THE ETERNAL ONE

"That Abraham was the one who
Mended the tear . . .
Between this world of men and
The Holy One blessed be He.
He brought people to the service of the living God.
He began to mend the rent pieces."

". . . וְלָמָּה נִקְרָא אָחוֹת שֶׁאָחָה אֶת הָעוֹלָם לִפְנֵי הקב״ה כָּאָדָם
הַזֶּה שֶׁקּוֹרֵעַ וּמְאַחֶה לְפִיכָךְ נִקְרָא אָחוֹת"

*Tanhuma
Lekh
Lekha
2*

You see, it was not so much that Abraham, our father
Understood that there was one God
But that he began to bring back His Presence.
To make us aware
Of the higher unity.
"Don't you see it," he would say
And we would see it — for a moment.
And then we would forget.
But this was enough to begin the return.
This was the real work of Abraham, our father.
Our progenitor, who at once did the only thing to be
Done and thereby presaged our task as well.

So the first Jew began being a Jew by mending the tear,
    restoring the intimate unity that we once
        shared with the Holy Ancient
           One of Old.

◆

PERSONAL NOTES

PERSONAL NOTES

PERSONAL NOTES

PERSONAL NOTES

PERSONAL NOTES

PERSONAL NOTES

PERSONAL NOTES

Children's Books

What You Will See Inside a Synagogue
By Rabbi Lawrence A. Hoffman and Dr. Ron Wolfson; Full-color photos by Bill Aron
A colorful, fun-to-read introduction that explains the ways and whys of Jewish worship and religious life. Full-page photos; concise but informative descriptions of the objects used, the clergy and laypeople who have specific roles, and much more. For ages 6 & up.

8½ x 10¼, 32 pp, Full-color photos, Hardcover, ISBN 1-59473-012-1 **$17.99** *(A SkyLight Paths book)*

Because Nothing Looks Like God
By Lawrence and Karen Kushner
What is God like? Introduces children to the possibilities of spiritual life. Real-life examples of happiness and sadness invite us to explore, together with our children, the questions we all have about God.

11 x 8½, 32 pp, Full-color illus., Hardcover, ISBN 1-58023-092-X **$16.95** *For ages 4 & up*

Also Available: **Because Nothing Looks Like God Teacher's Guide**
8½ x 11, 22 pp, PB, ISBN 1-58023-140-3 **$6.95** *For ages 5–8*

Board Book Companions to *Because Nothing Looks Like God*
5 x 5, 24 pp, Full-color illus., SkyLight Paths Board Books, **$7.95** each *For ages 0–4*

What Does God Look Like? ISBN 1-893361-23-3

How Does God Make Things Happen? ISBN 1-893361-24-1

Where Is God? ISBN 1-893361-17-9

The 11th Commandment: Wisdom from Our Children
by The Children of America
"If there were an Eleventh Commandment, what would it be?" Children of many religious denominations across America answer in their own drawings and words.
8 x 10, 48 pp, Full-color illus., Hardcover, ISBN 1-879045-46-X **$16.95** *For all ages*

Jerusalem of Gold: Jewish Stories of the Enchanted City
Retold by Howard Schwartz. Full-color illus. by Neil Waldman.
A beautiful and engaging collection of historical and legendary stories for children. Based on Talmud, midrash, Jewish folklore, and mystical and Hasidic sources.
8 x 10, 64 pp, Full-color illus., Hardcover, ISBN 1-58023-149-7 **$18.95** *For ages 7 & up*

The Book of Miracles: A Young Person's Guide to Jewish Spiritual Awareness
By Lawrence Kushner. All-new illustrations by the author.
6 x 9, 96 pp, 2-color illus., Hardcover, ISBN 1-879045-78-8 **$16.95** *For ages 9–13*

In Our Image: God's First Creatures
By Nancy Sohn Swartz
9 x 12, 32 pp, Full-color illus., Hardcover, ISBN 1-879045-99-0 **$16.95** *For ages 4 & up*

Also Available as a Board Book: **How Did the Animals Help God?**
5 x 5, 24 pp, Board, Full-color illus., ISBN 1-59473-044-X **$7.99** *For ages 0–4 (A SkyLight Paths book)*

From SKYLIGHT PATHS PUBLISHING

Becoming Me: A Story of Creation
By Martin Boroson. Full-color illus. by Christopher Gilvan-Cartwright.
Told in the personal "voice" of the Creator, a story about creation and relationship that is about each one of us.
8 x 10, 32 pp, Full-color illus., Hardcover, ISBN 1-893361-11-X **$16.95** *For ages 4 & up*

Ten Amazing People: And How They Changed the World
By Maura D. Shaw. Foreword by Dr. Robert Coles. Full-color illus. by Stephen Marchesi.
Black Elk • Dorothy Day • Malcolm X • Mahatma Gandhi • Martin Luther King, Jr. • Mother Teresa • Janusz Korczak • Desmond Tutu • Thich Nhat Hanh • Albert Schweitzer.
8½ x 11, 48 pp, Full-color illus., Hardcover, ISBN 1-893361-47-0 **$17.95** *For ages 7 & up*

Where Does God Live? *By August Gold and Matthew J. Perlman*
Helps young readers develop a personal understanding of God.
10 x 8½, 32 pp, Full-color photo illus., Quality PB, ISBN 1-893361-39-X **$8.99** *For ages 3–6*

Children's Books
by Sandy Eisenberg Sasso

Adam & Eve's First Sunset: God's New Day

Engaging new story explores fear and hope, faith and gratitude in ways that will delight kids and adults—inspiring us to bless each of God's days and nights.

9 x 12, 32 pp, Full-color illus., Hardcover, ISBN 1-58023-177-2 **$17.95** *For ages 4 & up*

But God Remembered

Stories of Women from Creation to the Promised Land

Four different stories of women—Lillith, Serach, Bityah, and the Daughters of Z—teach us important values through their faith and actions.

9 x 12, 32 pp, Full-color illus., Hardcover, ISBN 1-879045-43-5 **$16.95** *For ages 8 & up*

Cain & Abel: Finding the Fruits of Peace

Shows children that we have the power to deal with anger in positive ways. Provides questions for kids and adults to explore together.

9 x 12, 32 pp, Full-color illus., Hardcover, ISBN 1-58023-123-3 **$16.95** *For ages 5 & up*

God in Between

If you wanted to find God, where would you look? This magical, mythical tale teaches that God can be found where we are: within all of us and the relationships between us.

9 x 12, 32 pp, Full-color illus., Hardcover, ISBN 1-879045-86-9 **$16.95** *For ages 4 & up*

God's Paintbrush: Special 10th Anniversary Edition

Wonderfully interactive, invites children of all faiths and backgrounds to encounter God through moments in their own lives. Provides questions adult and child can explore together.

11 x 8½, 32 pp, Full-color illus., Hardcover, ISBN 1-58023-195-0 **$17.95** *For ages 4 & up*

Also Available: **God's Paintbrush Teacher's Guide**
8½ x 11, 32 pp, PB, ISBN 1-879045-57-5 **$8.95**

God's Paintbrush Celebration Kit

A Spiritual Activity Kit for Teachers and Students of All Faiths, All Backgrounds
Additional activity sheets available:
8-Student Activity Sheet Pack (40 sheets/5 sessions), ISBN 1-58023-058-X **$19.95**
Single-Student Activity Sheet Pack (5 sessions), ISBN 1-58023-059-8 **$3.95**

In God's Name

Like an ancient myth in its poetic text and vibrant illustrations, this award-winning modern fable about the search for God's name celebrates the diversity and, at the same time, the unity of all people.

9 x 12, 32 pp, Full-color illus., Hardcover, ISBN 1-879045-26-5 **$16.99** *For ages 4 & up*

Also Available as a Board Book: **What Is God's Name?**
5 x 5, 24 pp, Board, Full-color illus., ISBN 1-893361-10-1 **$7.99** *For ages 0–4 (A SkyLight Paths book)*

Also Available: **In God's Name video and study guide**
Computer animation, original music, and children's voices. 18 min. **$29.99**

Also Available in Spanish: **El nombre de Dios**
9 x 12, 32 pp, Full-color illus., Hardcover, ISBN 1-893361-63-2 **$16.95** *(A SkyLight Paths book)*

Noah's Wife: The Story of Naamah

When God tells Noah to bring the animals of the world onto the ark, God also calls on Naamah, Noah's wife, to save each plant on Earth. Based on an ancient text.

9 x 12, 32 pp, Full-color illus., Hardcover, ISBN 1-58023-134-9 **$16.95** *For ages 4 & up*

Also Available as a Board Book: **Naamah, Noah's Wife**
5 x 5, 24 pp, Full-color illus., Board, ISBN 1-893361-56-X **$7.95** *For ages 0–4 (A SkyLight Paths book)*

For Heaven's Sake: Finding God in Unexpected Places
9 x 12, 32 pp, Full-color illus., Hardcover, ISBN 1-58023-054-7 **$16.95** *For ages 4 & up*

God Said Amen: Finding the Answers to Our Prayers
9 x 12, 32 pp, Full-color illus., Hardcover, ISBN 1-58023-080-6 **$16.95** *For ages 4 & up*

Current Events/History

The Story of the Jews: A 4,000-Year Adventure—A Graphic History Book
Written & illustrated by Stan Mack
Witty, illustrated narrative of all the major happenings from biblical times to the twenty-first century. 6 x 9, 288 pp., illus., Quality PB, ISBN 1-58023-155-1 **$16.95**

Hannah Senesh: Her Life and Diary, the First Complete Edition
By Hannah Senesh; Foreword by Marge Piercy; Preface by Eitan Senesh
6 x 9, 352 pp., Hardcover, ISBN 1-58023-212-4 **$24.99**

The Jewish Prophet: Visionary Words from Moses and Miriam to Henrietta Szold and A. J. Heschel *By Rabbi Michael J. Shire*
6½ x 8½, 128 pp., 123 full-color illus., Hardcover, ISBN 1-58023-168-3 **Special gift price $14.95**

Shared Dreams: Martin Luther King, Jr. & the Jewish Community
By Rabbi Marc Schneier. Preface by Martin Luther King III.
6 x 9, 240 pp., Hardcover, ISBN 1-58023-062-8 **$24.95**

"Who Is a Jew?": Conversations, Not Conclusions *By Meryl Hyman*
6 x 9, 272 pp., Quality PB, ISBN 1-58023-052-0 **$16.95**

Ecology

Ecology & the Jewish Spirit: Where Nature & the Sacred Meet
Edited by Ellen Bernstein 6 x 9, 288 pp., Quality PB, ISBN 1-58023-082-2 **$16.95**

Torah of the Earth: Exploring 4,000 Years of Ecology in Jewish Thought
Vol. 1: Biblical Israel: One Land, One People; Rabbinic Judaism: One People, Many Lands
Vol. 2: Zionism: One Land, Two Peoples; Eco-Judaism: One Earth, Many Peoples
Edited by Rabbi Arthur Waskow
Vol. 1: 6 x 9, 272 pp., Quality PB, ISBN 1-58023-086-5 **$19.95**
Vol. 2: 6 x 9, 336 pp., Quality PB, ISBN 1-58023-087-3 **$19.95**

Grief/Healing

Against the Dying of the Light: A Parent's Story of Love, Loss and Hope
By Leonard Fein
Unusual exploration of heartbreak and healing. Chronicles the sudden death of author's 30-year-old daughter and shares the wisdom that emerges in the face of loss and grief.
5½ x 8½, 176 pp., Quality PB, ISBN 1-58023-197-7 **$15.99;** Hardcover, ISBN 1-58023-110-1 **$19.95**

Grief in Our Seasons: A Mourner's Kaddish Companion *By Rabbi Kerry M. Olitzky*
4½ x 6½, 448 pp., Quality PB, ISBN 1-879045-55-9 **$15.95**

Healing of Soul, Healing of Body: Spiritual Leaders Unfold the Strength & Solace in Psalms *Edited by Rabbi Simkha Y. Weintraub, C.S.W.*
6 x 9, 128 pp., 2-color illus. text, Quality PB, ISBN 1-879045-31-1 **$14.99**

Jewish Paths toward Healing and Wholeness: A Personal Guide to Dealing with Suffering *By Rabbi Kerry M. Olitzky. Foreword by Debbie Friedman.*
6 x 9, 192 pp., Quality PB, ISBN 1-58023-068-7 **$15.95**

Mourning & Mitzvah, 2nd Edition: A Guided Journal for Walking the Mourner's Path through Grief to Healing *By Anne Brener, L.C.S.W.*
7½ x 9, 304 pp., Quality PB, ISBN 1-58023-113-6 **$19.95**

The Perfect Stranger's Guide to Funerals and Grieving Practices
A Guide to Etiquette in Other People's Religious Ceremonies *Edited by Stuart M. Matlins*
6 x 9, 240 pp., Quality PB, ISBN 1-893361-20-9 **$16.95** *(A SkyLight Paths book)*

Tears of Sorrow, Seeds of Hope: A Jewish Spiritual Companion for Infertility and Pregnancy Loss *By Rabbi Nina Beth Cardin*
6 x 9, 192 pp., Hardcover, ISBN 1-58023-017-2 **$19.95**

A Time to Mourn, A Time to Comfort, 2nd Edition: A Guide to Jewish Bereavement and Comfort *By Dr. Ron Wolfson*
7 x 9, 336 pp., Quality PB, ISBN 1-58023-253-1 **$19.99**

When a Grandparent Dies: A Kid's Own Remembering Workbook for Dealing with Shiva and the Year Beyond *By Nechama Liss-Levinson, Ph.D.*
8 x 10, 48 pp., 2-color text, Hardcover, ISBN 1-879045-44-3 **$15.95** *For ages 7–13*

Abraham Joshua Heschel

The Earth Is the Lord's: The Inner World of the Jew in Eastern Europe
5½ x 8, 128 pp, Quality PB, ISBN 1-879045-42-7 **$14.95**

Israel: An Echo of Eternity *New Introduction by Susannah Heschel*
5½ x 8, 272 pp, Quality PB, ISBN 1-879045-70-2 **$19.95**

A Passion for Truth: Despair and Hope in Hasidism
5½ x 8, 352 pp, Quality PB, ISBN 1-879045-41-9 **$18.99**

Holidays/Holy Days

Leading the Passover Journey
The Seder's Meaning Revealed, the Haggadah's Story Retold
By Rabbi Nathan Laufer
Uncovers the hidden meaning of the Seder's rituals and customs
6 x 9, 208 pp, Hardcover, ISBN 1-58023-211-6 **$24.99**

Reclaiming Judaism as a Spiritual Practice: Holy Days and Shabbat
By Rabbi Goldie Milgram
Provides a framework for understanding the powerful and often unexplained intellectual, emotional, and spiritual tools that are essential for a lively, relevant, and fulfilling Jewish spiritual practice. 7 x 9, 272 pp, Quality PB, ISBN 1-58023-205-1 **$19.99**

7th Heaven: Celebrating Shabbat with Rebbe Nachman of Breslov
By Moshe Mykoff with the Breslov Research Institute
Explores the art of consciously observing Shabbat and understanding in-depth many of the day's spiritual practices. 5⅛ x 8¼, 224 pp, Deluxe PB w/flaps, ISBN 1-58023-175-6 **$18.95**

The Women's Passover Companion
Women's Reflections on the Festival of Freedom
Edited by Rabbi Sharon Cohen Anisfeld, Tara Mohr, and Catherine Spector
Groundbreaking. A provocative conversation about women's relationships to Passover as well as the roots and meanings of women's seders.
6 x 9, 352 pp, Hardcover, ISBN 1-58023-128-4 **$24.95**

The Women's Seder Sourcebook
Rituals & Readings for Use at the Passover Seder
Edited by Rabbi Sharon Cohen Anisfeld, Tara Mohr, and Catherine Spector
Gathers the voices of more than one hundred women in readings, personal and creative reflections, commentaries, blessings, and ritual suggestions that can be incorporated into your Passover celebration.
6 x 9, 384 pp, Hardcover, ISBN 1-58023-136-5 **$24.95**

Creating Lively Passover Seders: A Sourcebook of Engaging Tales, Texts & Activities
By David Arnow, Ph.D. 7 x 9, 416 pp, Quality PB, ISBN 1-58023-184-5 **$24.99**

Hanukkah, 2nd Edition: The Family Guide to Spiritual Celebration
By Dr. Ron Wolfson. Edited by Joel Lurie Grishaver.
7 x 9, 240 pp, illus., Quality PB, ISBN 1-58023-122-5 **$18.95**

The Jewish Family Fun Book: Holiday Projects, Everyday Activities, and Travel Ideas with Jewish Themes *By Danielle Dardashti and Roni Sarig. Illus. by Avi Katz.*
6 x 9, 288 pp, 70+ b/w illus. & diagrams, Quality PB, ISBN 1-58023-171-3 **$18.95**

The Jewish Gardening Cookbook: Growing Plants & Cooking for
Holidays & Festivals *By Michael Brown* 6 x 9, 224 pp, 30+ illus., Quality PB, ISBN 1-58023-116-0 **$16.95**

The Jewish Lights Book of Fun Classroom Activities: Simple and Seasonal Projects for Teachers and Students *By Danielle Dardashti and Roni Sarig*
6 x 9, 240 pp, Quality PB, ISBN 1-58023-206-X **$19.99**

Passover, 2nd Edition: The Family Guide to Spiritual Celebration
By Dr. Ron Wolfson with Joel Lurie Grishaver 7 x 9, 352 pp, Quality PB, ISBN 1-58023-174-8 **$19.95**

Shabbat, 2nd Edition: The Family Guide to Preparing for and Celebrating the Sabbath
By Dr. Ron Wolfson 7 x 9, 320 pp, illus., Quality PB, ISBN 1-58023-164-0 **$19.95**

Sharing Blessings: Children's Stories for Exploring the Spirit of the Jewish Holidays
By Rahel Musleah and Michael Klayman
8½ x 11, 64 pp, Full-color illus., Hardcover, ISBN 1-879045-71-0 **$18.95** *For ages 6 & up*

Life Cycle

Marriage / Parenting / Family / Aging

Jewish Fathers: A Legacy of Love
Photographs by Lloyd Wolf. Essays by Paula Wolfson. Foreword by Harold S. Kushner.
Honors the role of contemporary Jewish fathers in America. Each father tells in his own words what it means to be a parent and Jewish, and what he learned from his own father. Insightful photos. 9½ x 9⅞, 144 pp with 100+ duotone photos, Hardcover, ISBN 1-58023-204-3 **$30.00**

The New Jewish Baby Album: Creating and Celebrating the Beginning of a Spiritual Life—A Jewish Lights Companion
By the Editors at Jewish Lights. Foreword by Anita Diamant. Preface by Sandy Eisenberg Sasso.
A spiritual keepsake that will be treasured for generations. More than just a memory book, *shows you how—and why it's important*—to create a Jewish home and a Jewish life. 8 x 10, 64 pp, Deluxe Padded Hardcover, Full-color illus., ISBN 1-58023-138-1 **$19.95**

The Jewish Pregnancy Book: A Resource for the Soul, Body & Mind during Pregnancy, Birth & the First Three Months
By Sandy Falk, M.D., and Rabbi Daniel Judson, with Steven A. Rapp
Includes medical information, prayers and rituals for each stage of pregnancy, from a liberal Jewish perspective. 7 x 10, 208 pp, Quality PB, b/w illus., ISBN 1-58023-178-0 **$16.95**

Celebrating Your New Jewish Daughter: Creating Jewish Ways to Welcome Baby Girls into the Covenant—New and Traditional Ceremonies
By Debra Nussbaum Cohen 6 x 9, 272 pp, Quality PB, ISBN 1-58023-090-3 **$18.95**

The New Jewish Baby Book, 2nd Edition: Names, Ceremonies & Customs—A Guide for Today's Families *By Anita Diamant* 6 x 9, 336 pp, Quality PB, ISBN 1-58023-251-5 **$19.99**

Parenting As a Spiritual Journey: Deepening Ordinary and Extraordinary Events into Sacred Occasions *By Rabbi Nancy Fuchs-Kreimer* 6 x 9, 224 pp, Quality PB, ISBN 1-58023-016-4 **$16.95**

Judaism for Two: A Spiritual Guide for Strengthening and Celebrating Your Loving Relationship *By Rabbi Nancy Fuchs-Kreimer and Rabbi Nancy H. Wiener*
Addresses the ways Jewish teachings can enhance and strengthen committed relationships. 6 x 9, 208 pp, Quality PB, ISBN 1-58023-254-X **$16.99**

Embracing the Covenant: Converts to Judaism Talk About Why & How
By Rabbi Allan Berkowitz and Patti Moskovitz 6 x 9, 192 pp, Quality PB, ISBN 1-879045-50-8 **$16.95**

The Guide to Jewish Interfaith Family Life: An InterfaithFamily.com Handbook
Edited by Ronnie Friedland and Edmund Case 6 x 9, 384 pp, Quality PB, ISBN 1-58023-153-5 **$18.95**

Introducing My Faith and My Community
The Jewish Outreach Institute Guide for the Christian in a Jewish Interfaith Relationship
By Rabbi Kerry M. Olitzky 6 x 9, 176 pp, Quality PB, ISBN 1-58023-192-6 **$16.99**

Making a Successful Jewish Interfaith Marriage: The Jewish Outreach Institute Guide to Opportunities, Challenges and Resources
By Rabbi Kerry M. Olitzky with Joan Peterson Littman 6 x 9, 176 pp, Quality PB, ISBN 1-58023-170-5 **$16.95**

The Creative Jewish Wedding Book: A Hands-On Guide to New & Old Traditions, Ceremonies & Celebrations *By Gabrielle Kaplan-Mayer*
Provides the tools to create the most meaningful Jewish traditional or alternative wedding by using ritual elements to express your unique style and spirituality. 9 x 9, 288 pp, b/w photos, Quality PB, ISBN 1-58023-194-2 **$19.99**

Divorce Is a Mitzvah: A Practical Guide to Finding Wholeness and Holiness When Your Marriage Dies *By Rabbi Perry Netter. Afterword by Rabbi Laura Geller.*
6 x 9, 224 pp, Quality PB, ISBN 1-58023-172-1 **$16.95**

A Heart of Wisdom: Making the Jewish Journey from Midlife through the Elder Years
Edited by Susan Berrin. Foreword by Harold Kushner. 6 x 9, 384 pp, Quality PB, ISBN 1-58023-051-2 **$18.95**

So That Your Values Live On: Ethical Wills and How to Prepare Them
Edited by Jack Riemer and Nathaniel Stampfer 6 x 9, 272 pp, Quality PB, ISBN 1-879045-34-6 **$18.95**

Meditation

The Handbook of Jewish Meditation Practices
A Guide for Enriching the Sabbath and Other Days of Your Life
By Rabbi David A. Cooper
Easy-to-learn meditation techniques. 6 x 9, 208 pp, Quality PB, ISBN 1-58023-102-0 **$16.95**

Discovering Jewish Meditation: Instruction & Guidance for Learning an Ancient
Spiritual Practice *By Nan Fink Gefen, Ph.D.* 6 x 9, 208 pp, Quality PB, ISBN 1-58023-067-9 **$16.95**

A Heart of Stillness: A Complete Guide to Learning the Art of Meditation
By Rabbi David A. Cooper 5½ x 8½, 272 pp, Quality PB, ISBN 1-893361-03-9 **$16.95**
(A SkyLight Paths book)

Meditation from the Heart of Judaism: Today's Teachers Share Their
Practices, Techniques, and Faith *Edited by Avram Davis*
6 x 9, 256 pp, Quality PB, ISBN 1-58023-049-0 **$16.95**

Silence, Simplicity & Solitude: A Complete Guide to Spiritual Retreat at Home
By Rabbi David A. Cooper 5½ x 8½, 336 pp, Quality PB, ISBN 1-893361-04-7 **$16.95**
(A SkyLight Paths book)

The Way of Flame: A Guide to the Forgotten Mystical Tradition of Jewish
Meditation *By Avram Davis* 4½ x 8, 176 pp, Quality PB, ISBN 1-58023-060-1 **$15.95**

Ritual/Sacred Practice/Journaling

The Jewish Dream Book: The Key to Opening the Inner Meaning of
Your Dreams *By Vanessa L. Ochs with Elizabeth Ochs; Full-color illus. by Kristina Swarner*
Instructions for how modern people can perform ancient Jewish dream practices
and dream interpretations drawn from the Jewish wisdom tradition. For anyone
who wants to understand their dreams—and themselves.
8 x 8, 120 pp, Full-color illus., Deluxe PB w/flaps, ISBN 1-58023-132-2 **$16.95**

The Jewish Journaling Book: How to Use Jewish Tradition to Write
Your Life & Explore Your Soul *By Janet Ruth Falon*
Details the history of Jewish journaling throughout biblical and modern times,
and teaches specific journaling techniques to help you create and maintain a vital
journal, from a Jewish perspective. 8 x 8, 304 pp, Deluxe PB w/flaps, ISBN 1-58023-203-5 **$18.99**

The Book of Jewish Sacred Practices: CLAL's Guide to Everyday & Holiday
Rituals & Blessings *Edited by Rabbi Irwin Kula and Vanessa L. Ochs, Ph.D.*
6 x 9, 368 pp, Quality PB, ISBN 1-58023-152-7 **$18.95**

Jewish Ritual: A Brief Introduction for Christians
By Rabbi Kerry M. Olitzky and Rabbi Daniel Judson
5½ x 8½, 144 pp, Quality PB, ISBN 1-58023-210-8 **$14.99**

The Rituals & Practices of a Jewish Life: A Handbook for Personal Spiritual
Renewal *Edited by Rabbi Kerry M. Olitzky and Rabbi Daniel Judson*
6 x 9, 272 pp, illus., Quality PB, ISBN 1-58023-169-1 **$18.95**

Science Fiction/ Mystery & Detective Fiction

Mystery Midrash: An Anthology of Jewish Mystery & Detective Fiction
Edited by Lawrence W. Raphael. Preface by Joel Siegel.
6 x 9, 304 pp, Quality PB, ISBN 1-58023-055-5 **$16.95**

Criminal Kabbalah: An Intriguing Anthology of Jewish Mystery & Detective Fiction
Edited by Lawrence W. Raphael. Foreword by Laurie R. King.
6 x 9, 256 pp, Quality PB, ISBN 1-58023-109-8 **$16.95**

More Wandering Stars: An Anthology of Outstanding Stories of Jewish Fantasy and
Science Fiction *Edited by Jack Dann. Introduction by Isaac Asimov.*
6 x 9, 192 pp, Quality PB, ISBN 1-58023-063-6 **$16.95**

Wandering Stars: An Anthology of Jewish Fantasy & Science Fiction
Edited by Jack Dann. Introduction by Isaac Asimov.
6 x 9, 272 pp, Quality PB, ISBN 1-58023-005-9 **$16.95**

Spirituality

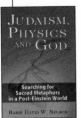

Does the Soul Survive?: A Jewish Journey to Belief in Afterlife, Past Lives & Living with Purpose   *By Rabbi Elie Kaplan Spitz. Foreword by Brian L. Weiss, M.D.*
Spitz relates his own experiences and those shared with him by people he has worked with as a rabbi, and shows us that belief in afterlife and past lives, so often approached with reluctance, is in fact true to Jewish tradition.
6 x 9, 288 pp, Quality PB, ISBN 1-58023-165-9 **$16.95**; Hardcover, ISBN 1-58023-094-6 **$21.95**

First Steps to a New Jewish Spirit: Reb Zalman's Guide to Recapturing the Intimacy & Ecstasy in Your Relationship with God
By Rabbi Zalman M. Schachter-Shalomi with Donald Gropman
An extraordinary spiritual handbook that restores psychic and physical vigor by introducing us to new models and alternative ways of practicing Judaism. Offers meditation and contemplation exercises for enriching the most important aspects of everyday life.   6 x 9, 144 pp, Quality PB, ISBN 1-58023-182-9 **$16.95**

God in Our Relationships: Spirituality between People from the Teachings of Martin Buber   *By Rabbi Dennis S. Ross*
On the eightieth anniversary of Buber's classic work, we can discover new answers to critical issues in our lives. Inspiring examples from Ross's own life— as congregational rabbi, father, hospital chaplain, social worker, and husband— illustrate Buber's difficult-to-understand ideas about how we encounter God and each other. 5½ x 8½, 160 pp, Quality PB, ISBN 1-58023-147-0 **$16.95**

Judaism, Physics and God: Searching for Sacred Metaphors in a Post-Einstein World   *By Rabbi David W. Nelson*
In clear, non-technical terms, this provocative fusion of religion and science examines the great theories of modern physics to find new ways for contemporary people to express their spiritual beliefs and thoughts.
6 x 9, 352 pp, Hardcover, ISBN 1-58023-252-3 **$24.99**

The Jewish Lights Spirituality Handbook: A Guide to Understanding, Exploring & Living a Spiritual Life   *Edited by Stuart M. Matlins*
What exactly is "Jewish" about spirituality? How do I make it a part of my life? Fifty of today's foremost spiritual leaders share their ideas and experience with us.
6 x 9, 456 pp, Quality PB, ISBN 1-58023-093-8 **$19.95**; Hardcover, ISBN 1-58023-100-4 **$24.95**

Bringing the Psalms to Life: How to Understand and Use the Book of Psalms
By Dr. Daniel F. Polish
6 x 9, 208 pp, Quality PB, ISBN 1-58023-157-8 **$16.95**; Hardcover, ISBN 1-58023-077-6 **$21.95**

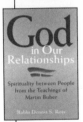

God & the Big Bang: Discovering Harmony between Science & Spirituality
By Dr. Daniel C. Matt 6 x 9, 216 pp, Quality PB, ISBN 1-879045-89-3 **$16.95**

Godwrestling—Round 2: Ancient Wisdom, Future Paths
By Rabbi Arthur Waskow 6 x 9, 352 pp, Quality PB, ISBN 1-879045-72-9 **$18.95**

One God Clapping: The Spiritual Path of a Zen Rabbi   *By Rabbi Alan Lew with Sherril Jaffe*
5½ x 8½, 336 pp, Quality PB, ISBN 1-58023-115-2 **$16.95**

The Path of Blessing: Experiencing the Energy and Abundance of the Divine
By Rabbi Marcia Prager 5½ x 8½, 240 pp., Quality PB, ISBN 1-58023-148-9 **$16.95**

Six Jewish Spiritual Paths: A Rationalist Looks at Spirituality   *By Rabbi Rifat Sonsino*
6 x 9, 208 pp, Quality PB, ISBN 1-58023-167-5 **$16.95**; Hardcover, ISBN 1-58023-095-4 **$21.95**

Soul Judaism: Dancing with God into a New Era
By Rabbi Wayne Dosick 5½ x 8½, 304 pp, Quality PB, ISBN 1-58023-053-9 **$16.95**

Stepping Stones to Jewish Spiritual Living: Walking the Path Morning, Noon, and Night   *By Rabbi James L. Mirel and Karen Bonnell Werth*
6 x 9, 240 pp, Quality PB, ISBN 1-58023-074-1 **$16.95**; Hardcover, ISBN 1-58023-003-2 **$21.95**

There Is No Messiah... and You're It: The Stunning Transformation of Judaism's Most Provocative Idea   *By Rabbi Robert N. Levine, D.D.*
6 x 9, 192 pp, Quality PB, ISBN 1-58023-255-8 **$16.99**; Hardcover, ISBN 1-58023-173-X **$21.95**

These Are the Words: A Vocabulary of Jewish Spiritual Life   *By Dr. Arthur Green*
6 x 9, 304 pp, Quality PB, ISBN 1-58023-107-1 **$18.95**

Spirituality/Women's Interest

The Quotable Jewish Woman: Wisdom, Inspiration & Humor from the Mind & Heart *Edited and compiled by Elaine Bernstein Partnow*
The definitive collection of ideas, reflections, humor, and wit of over 300 Jewish women.
6 x 9, 496 pp, Hardcover, ISBN 1-58023-193-4 **$29.99**

Lifecycles, Vol. 1: Jewish Women on Life Passages & Personal Milestones
Edited and with introductions by Rabbi Debra Orenstein 6 x 9, 480 pp, Quality PB, ISBN 1-58023-018-0 **$19.95**

Lifecycles, Vol. 2: Jewish Women on Biblical Themes in Contemporary Life
Edited and with introductions by Rabbi Debra Orenstein and Rabbi Jane Rachel Litman
6 x 9, 464 pp, Quality PB, ISBN 1-58023-019-9 **$19.95**

Moonbeams: A Hadassah Rosh Hodesh Guide *Edited by Carol Diament, Ph.D.*
8½ x 11, 240 pp, Quality PB, ISBN 1-58023-099-7 **$20.00**

ReVisions: Seeing Torah through a Feminist Lens *By Rabbi Elyse Goldstein*
5½ x 8½, 224 pp, Quality PB, ISBN 1-58023-117-9 **$16.95**

White Fire: A Portrait of Women Spiritual Leaders in America
By Rabbi Malka Drucker. Photographs by Gay Block.
7 x 10, 320 pp, 30+ b/w photos, Hardcover, ISBN 1-893361-64-0 **$24.95** *(A SkyLight Paths book)*

Women of the Wall: Claiming Sacred Ground at Judaism's Holy Site
Edited by Phyllis Chesler and Rivka Haut 6 x 9, 496 pp, b/w photos, Hardcover, ISBN 1-58023-161-6 **$34.95**

The Women's Haftarah Commentary: New Insights from Women Rabbis on the 54 Weekly Haftarah Portions, the 5 Megillot & Special Shabbatot
Edited by Rabbi Elyse Goldstein 6 x 9, 560 pp, Hardcover, ISBN 1-58023-133-0 **$39.99**

The Women's Torah Commentary: New Insights from Women Rabbis on the 54 Weekly Torah Portions *Edited by Rabbi Elyse Goldstein*
6 x 9, 496 pp, Hardcover, ISBN 1-58023-076-8 **$34.95**

The Year Mom Got Religion: One Woman's Midlife Journey into Judaism
By Lee Meyerhoff Hendler 6 x 9, 208 pp, Quality PB, ISBN 1-58023-070-9 **$15.95**

See Holidays for *The Women's Passover Companion: Women's Reflections on the Festival of Freedom* and *The Women's Seder Sourcebook: Rituals & Readings for Use at the Passover Seder.* Also see Bar/Bat Mitzvah for *The JGirl's Guide: The Young Jewish Woman's Handbook for Coming of Age.*

Travel

Israel—A Spiritual Travel Guide, 2nd Edition
A Companion for the Modern Jewish Pilgrim
By Rabbi Lawrence A. Hoffman 4¾ x 10, 256 pp, Quality PB, illus., ISBN 1-58023-261-2 **$18.99**
Also Available: **The Israel Mission Leader's Guide** ISBN 1-58023-085-7 **$4.95**

12 Steps

100 Blessings Every Day Daily Twelve Step Recovery Affirmations, Exercises for Personal Growth & Renewal Reflecting Seasons of the Jewish Year
By Rabbi Kerry M. Olitzky. Foreword by Rabbi Neil Gillman.
One-day-at-a-time monthly format. Reflects on the rhythm of the Jewish calendar to bring insight to recovery from addictions.
4½ x 6½, 432 pp, Quality PB, ISBN 1-879045-30-3 **$15.99**

Recovery from Codependence: A Jewish Twelve Steps Guide to Healing Your Soul
By Rabbi Kerry M. Olitzky 6 x 9, 160 pp, Quality PB, ISBN 1-879045-32-X **$13.95**

Renewed Each Day: Daily Twelve Step Recovery Meditations Based on the Bible
By Rabbi Kerry M. Olitzky and Aaron Z.
Vol. 1—Genesis & Exodus: 6 x 9, 224 pp, Quality PB, ISBN 1-879045-12-5 **$14.95**
Vol. 2—Leviticus, Numbers & Deuteronomy: 6 x 9, 280 pp, Quality PB, ISBN 1-879045-13-3 **$14.95**

Twelve Jewish Steps to Recovery: A Personal Guide to Turning from Alcoholism & Other Addictions—Drugs, Food, Gambling, Sex...
By Rabbi Kerry M. Olitzky and Stuart A. Copans, M.D. Preface by Abraham J. Twerski, M.D.
6 x 9, 144 pp, Quality PB, ISBN 1-879045-09-5 **$14.95**

Theology/Philosophy

Aspects of Rabbinic Theology
By Solomon Schechter. New Introduction by Dr. Neil Gillman.
6 x 9, 448 pp, Quality PB, ISBN 1-879045-24-9 **$19.95**

Broken Tablets: Restoring the Ten Commandments and Ourselves
Edited by Rachel S. Mikva. Introduction by Lawrence Kushner. Afterword by Arnold Jacob Wolf.
6 x 9, 192 pp, Quality PB, ISBN 1-58023-158-6 **$16.95**; Hardcover, ISBN 1-58023-066-0 **$21.95**

Creating an Ethical Jewish Life
A Practical Introduction to Classic Teachings on How to Be a Jew
By Dr. Byron L. Sherwin and Seymour J. Cohen
6 x 9, 336 pp, Quality PB, ISBN 1-58023-114-4 **$19.95**

The Death of Death: Resurrection and Immortality in Jewish Thought
By Dr. Neil Gillman 6 x 9, 336 pp, Quality PB, ISBN 1-58023-081-4 **$18.95**

Evolving Halakhah: A Progressive Approach to Traditional Jewish Law
By Rabbi Dr. Moshe Zemer
6 x 9, 480 pp, Quality PB, ISBN 1-58023-127-6 **$29.95**; Hardcover, ISBN 1-58023-002-4 **$40.00**

Hasidic Tales: Annotated & Explained
By Rabbi Rami Shapiro. Foreword by Andrew Harvey, SkyLight Illuminations series editor.
5½ x 8½, 240 pp, Quality PB, ISBN 1-893361-86-1 **$16.95** *(A SkyLight Paths Book)*

A Heart of Many Rooms: Celebrating the Many Voices within Judaism
By Dr. David Hartman 6 x 9, 352 pp, Quality PB, ISBN 1-58023-156-X **$19.95**

The Hebrew Prophets: Selections Annotated & Explained
Translation & Annotation by Rabbi Rami Shapiro. Foreword by Zalman M. Schachter-Shalomi
5½ x 8½, 224 pp, Quality PB, ISBN 1-59473-037-7 **$16.99** *(A SkyLight Paths book)*

Keeping Faith with the Psalms: Deepen Your Relationship with God Using the Book of Psalms *By Daniel F. Polish* 6 x 9, 272 pp, Hardcover, ISBN 1-58023-179-9 **$24.95**

The Last Trial
On the Legends and Lore of the Command to Abraham to Offer Isaac as a Sacrifice
By Shalom Spiegel. New Introduction by Judah Goldin.
6 x 9, 208 pp, Quality PB, ISBN 1-879045-29-X **$18.95**

A Living Covenant: The Innovative Spirit in Traditional Judaism
By Dr. David Hartman 6 x 9, 368 pp, Quality PB, ISBN 1-58023-011-3 **$18.95**

Love and Terror in the God Encounter
The Theological Legacy of Rabbi Joseph B. Soloveitchik
By Dr. David Hartman
6 x 9, 240 pp, Quality PB, ISBN 1-58023-176-4 **$19.95**; Hardcover, ISBN 1-58023-112-8 **$25.00**

Seeking the Path to Life
Theological Meditations on God and the Nature of People, Love, Life and Death
By Rabbi Ira F. Stone 6 x 9, 160 pp, Quality PB, ISBN 1-879045-47-8 **$14.95**

The Spirit of Renewal: Finding Faith after the Holocaust
By Rabbi Edward Feld 6 x 9, 224 pp, Quality PB, ISBN 1-879045-40-0 **$16.95**

Tormented Master: *The Life and Spiritual Quest of Rabbi Nahman of Bratslav*
By Dr. Arthur Green 6 x 9, 416 pp, Quality PB, ISBN 1-879045-11-7 **$19.99**

Your Word Is Fire: The Hasidic Masters on Contemplative Prayer
Edited and translated by Dr. Arthur Green and Barry W. Holtz
6 x 9, 160 pp, Quality PB, ISBN 1-879045-25-7 **$15.95**

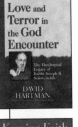

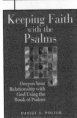

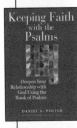

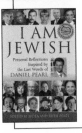

I Am Jewish
Personal Reflections Inspired by the Last Words of Daniel Pearl
Almost 150 Jews—both famous and not—from all walks of life, from all around the world, write about Identity, Heritage, Covenant / Chosenness and Faith, Humanity and Ethnicity, and *Tikkun Olam* and Justice.
Edited by Judea and Ruth Pearl
6 x 9, 304 pp, Deluxe PB w/flaps, ISBN 1-58023-259-0 **$18.99**; Hardcover, ISBN 1-58023-183-7 **$24.99**
Download a free copy of the *I Am Jewish Teacher's Guide* at our website:
www.jewishlights.com

Spirituality/The Way Into... Series

The Way Into... Series offers an accessible and highly usable "guided tour" of the Jewish faith, people, history and beliefs—in total, an introduction to Judaism that will enable you to understand and interact with the sacred texts of the Jewish tradition. Each volume is written by a leading contemporary scholar and teacher, and explores one key aspect of Judaism. *The Way Into...* enables all readers to achieve a real sense of Jewish cultural literacy through guided study.

The Way Into Encountering God in Judaism *By Neil Gillman*
6 x 9, 240 pp, Quality PB, ISBN 1-58023-199-3 **$18.99**; Hardcover, ISBN 1-58023-025-3 **$21.95**

Also Available: **The Jewish Approach to God: A Brief Introduction for Christians**
By Neil Gillman 5½ x 8¼, 192 pp, Quality PB, ISBN 1-58023-190-X **$16.95**

The Way Into Jewish Mystical Tradition *By Lawrence Kushner*
6 x 9, 224 pp, Quality PB, ISBN 1-58023-200-0 **$18.99**; Hardcover, ISBN 1-58023-029-6 **$21.95**

The Way Into Jewish Prayer *By Lawrence A. Hoffman*
6 x 9, 224 pp, Quality PB, ISBN 1-58023-201-9 **$18.99**; Hardcover, ISBN 1-58023-027-X **$21.95**

The Way Into Torah *By Norman J. Cohen*
6 x 9, 176 pp, Quality PB, ISBN 1-58023-198-5 **$16.99**; Hardcover, ISBN 1-58023-028-8 **$21.95**

  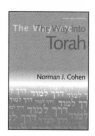

Spirituality in the Workplace

Being God's Partner
How to Find the Hidden Link Between Spirituality and Your Work
By Rabbi Jeffrey K. Salkin. Introduction by Norman Lear.
6 x 9, 192 pp, Quality PB, ISBN 1-879045-65-6 **$17.95**

The Business Bible: 10 New Commandments for Bringing Spirituality & Ethical Values into the Workplace *By Rabbi Wayne Dosick*
5½ x 8¼, 208 pp, Quality PB, ISBN 1-58023-101-2 **$14.95**

Spirituality and Wellness

Aleph-Bet Yoga
Embodying the Hebrew Letters for Physical and Spiritual Well-Being
By Steven A. Rapp. Foreword by Tamar Frankiel, Ph.D., and Judy Greenfeld. Preface by Hart Lazer
7 x 10, 128 pp, b/w photos, Quality PB, Layflat binding, ISBN 1-58023-162-4 **$16.95**

Entering the Temple of Dreams
Jewish Prayers, Movements, and Meditations for the End of the Day
By Tamar Frankiel, Ph.D., and Judy Greenfeld
7 x 10, 192 pp, illus., Quality PB, ISBN 1-58023-079-2 **$16.95**

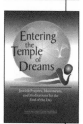

Jewish Paths toward Healing and Wholeness: A Personal Guide to Dealing with Suffering *By Rabbi Kerry M. Olitzky. Foreword by Debbie Friedman.*
6 x 9, 192 pp, Quality PB, ISBN 1-58023-068-7 **$15.95**

Minding the Temple of the Soul
Balancing Body, Mind, and Spirit through Traditional Jewish Prayer, Movement, and Meditation *By Tamar Frankiel, Ph.D., and Judy Greenfeld*
7 x 10, 184 pp, illus., Quality PB, ISBN 1-879045-64-8 **$16.95**
Audiotape of the Blessings and Meditations: 60 min. **$9.95**
Videotape of the Movements and Meditations: 46 min. **$20.00**

Inspiration

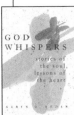

God in All Moments
Mystical & Practical Spiritual Wisdom from Hasidic Masters
Edited and translated by Or N. Rose with Ebn D. Leader
Hasidic teachings on how to be mindful in religious practice and cultivating every-day ethical behavior—*hanhagot.* 5½ x 8¼, 192 pp, Quality PB, ISBN 1-58023-186-1 **$16.95**

Our Dance with God: Finding Prayer, Perspective and Meaning in the
Stories of Our Lives *By Karyn D. Kedar*
Inspiring spiritual insight to guide you on your life journeys and teach you to live and thrive in two conflicting worlds: the rational/material and the spiritual.
6 x 9, 176 pp, Quality PB, ISBN 1-58023-202-7 **$16.99**

Also Available: **The Dance of the Dolphin** (Hardcover edition of *Our Dance with God*)
6 x 9, 176 pp, Hardcover, ISBN 1-58023-154-3 **$19.95**

The Empty Chair: Finding Hope and Joy—Timeless Wisdom from a Hasidic Master,
Rebbe Nachman of Breslov *Adapted by Moshe Mykoff and the Breslov Research Institute*
4 x 6, 128 pp, 2-color text, Deluxe PB w/flaps, ISBN 1-879045-67-2 **$9.95**

The Gentle Weapon: Prayers for Everyday and Not-So-Everyday Moments—
Timeless Wisdom from the Teachings of the Hasidic Master, Rebbe Nachman of Breslov
Adapted by Moshe Mykoff and S. C. Mizrahi, together with the Breslov Research Institute
4 x 6, 144 pp, 2-color text, Deluxe PB w/flaps, ISBN 1-58023-022-9 **$9.95**

God Whispers: Stories of the Soul, Lessons of the Heart *By Karyn D. Kedar*
6 x 9, 176 pp, Quality PB, ISBN 1-58023-088-1 **$15.95**

An Orphan in History: One Man's Triumphant Search for His Jewish Roots
By Paul Cowan. Afterword by Rachel Cowan. 6 x 9, 288 pp, Quality PB, ISBN 1-58023-135-7 **$16.95**

Restful Reflections: Nighttime Inspiration to Calm the Soul, Based on Jewish Wisdom
By Rabbi Kerry M. Olitzky & Rabbi Lori Forman 4½ x 6¼, 448 pp, Quality PB, ISBN 1-58023-091-1 **$15.95**

Sacred Intentions: Daily Inspiration to Strengthen the Spirit, Based on Jewish Wisdom
By Rabbi Kerry M. Olitzky and Rabbi Lori Forman 4½ x 6¼, 448 pp, Quality PB, ISBN 1-58023-061-X **$15.95**

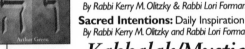

Kabbalah/Mysticism/Enneagram

Seek My Face: A Jewish Mystical Theology
By Dr. Arthur Green
This classic work of contemporary Jewish theology, revised and updated, is a profound, deeply personal statement of the lasting truths of Jewish mysticism and the basic faith claims of Judaism. A tool for anyone seeking the elusive presence of God in the world. 6 x 9, 304 pp, Quality PB, ISBN 1-58023-130-6 **$19.95**

Zohar: Annotated & Explained
Translation and annotation by Dr. Daniel C. Matt. Foreword by Andrew Harvey
Offers insightful yet unobtrusive commentary to the masterpiece of Jewish mysticism. Explains references and mystical symbols, shares wisdom of spiritual masters, and clarifies the *Zohar*'s bold claim: We have always been taught that we need God, but in order to manifest in the world, God needs us.
5½ x 8¼, 160 pp, Quality PB, ISBN 1-893361-51-9 **$15.99** *(A SkyLight Paths book)*

Cast in God's Image: Discover Your Personality Type Using the Enneagram and Kabbalah
By Rabbi Howard A. Addison
7 x 9, 176 pp, Quality PB, Layflat binding, 20+ journaling exercises, ISBN 1-58023-124-1 **$16.95**

Ehyeh: A Kabbalah for Tomorrow *By Dr. Arthur Green*
6 x 9, 224 pp, Quality PB, ISBN 1-58023-213-2 **$16.99**; Hardcover, ISBN 1-58023-125-X **$21.95**

The Enneagram and Kabbalah: Reading Your Soul *By Rabbi Howard A. Addison*
6 x 9, 176 pp, Quality PB, ISBN 1-58023-001-6 **$15.95**

Finding Joy: A Practical Spiritual Guide to Happiness *By Dannel I. Schwartz with Mark Hass*
6 x 9, 192 pp, Quality PB, ISBN 1-58023-009-1 **$14.95**

The Gift of Kabbalah: Discovering the Secrets of Heaven, Renewing Your Life on Earth
By Tamar Frankiel, Ph.D.
6 x 9, 256 pp, Quality PB, ISBN 1-58023-141-1 **$16.95**; Hardcover, ISBN 1-58023-108-X **$21.95**

The Way Into Jewish Mystical Tradition *By Lawrence Kushner*
6 x 9, 224 pp, Quality PB, ISBN 1-58023-200-0 **$18.99**; Hardcover, ISBN 1-58023-029-6 **$21.95**

Spirituality/Lawrence Kushner

Filling Words with Light: Hasidic and Mystical Reflections on Jewish Prayer
By Lawrence Kushner and Nehemia Polen
Reflects on the joy, gratitude, mystery, and awe embedded in traditional prayers and blessings, and shows how you can imbue these familiar sacred words with your own sense of holiness.   5½ x 8¼, 176 pp, Hardcover, ISBN 1-58023-216-7 **$21.99**

The Book of Letters: A Mystical Hebrew Alphabet
Popular Hardcover Edition, 6 x 9, 80 pp, 2-color text, ISBN 1-879045-00-1 **$24.95**
Collector's Limited Edition, 9 x 12, 80 pp, gold foil embossed pages, w/limited edition silkscreened print, ISBN 1-879045-04-4 **$349.00**

The Book of Miracles: A Young Person's Guide to Jewish Spiritual Awareness
6 x 9, 96 pp, 2-color illus., Hardcover, ISBN 1-879045-78-8 **$16.95** *For ages 9–13*

The Book of Words: Talking Spiritual Life, Living Spiritual Talk
6 x 9, 160 pp, Quality PB, ISBN 1-58023-020-2 **$16.95**

Eyes Remade for Wonder: A Lawrence Kushner Reader   *Introduction by Thomas Moore*
6 x 9, 240 pp, Quality PB, ISBN 1-58023-042-3 **$18.95**; Hardcover, ISBN 1-58023-014-8 **$23.95**

God Was in This Place & I, i Did Not Know
Finding Self, Spirituality and Ultimate Meaning   6 x 9, 192 pp, Quality PB, ISBN 1-879045-33-8 **$16.95**

Honey from the Rock: An Introduction to Jewish Mysticism
6 x 9, 176 pp, Quality PB, ISBN 1-58023-073-3 **$16.95**

Invisible Lines of Connection: Sacred Stories of the Ordinary
5½ x 8½, 160 pp, Quality PB, ISBN 1-879045-98-2 **$15.95**

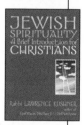

Jewish Spirituality—A Brief Introduction for Christians
5½ x 8½, 112 pp, Quality PB Original, ISBN 1-58023-150-0 **$12.95**

The River of Light: Jewish Mystical Awareness   6 x 9, 192 pp, Quality PB, ISBN 1-58023-096-2 **$16.95**

The Way Into Jewish Mystical Tradition
6 x 9, 224 pp, Quality PB, ISBN 1-58023-200-0 **$18.99**; Hardcover, ISBN 1-58023-029-6 **$21.95**

Spirituality/Prayer

Pray Tell: A Hadassah Guide to Jewish Prayer
By Rabbi Jules Harlow, with contributions from Tamara Cohen, Rochelle Furstenberg, Rabbi Daniel Gordis, Leora Tanenbaum, and many others
A guide to traditional Jewish prayer enriched with insight and wisdom from a broad variety of viewpoints—from Orthodox, Conservative, Reform, and Reconstructionist Judaism to New Age and feminist.
8½ x 11, 400 pp, Quality PB, ISBN 1-58023-163-2 **$29.95**

My People's Prayer Book Series
Traditional Prayers, Modern Commentaries   *Edited by Rabbi Lawrence A. Hoffman*
Provides diverse and exciting commentary to the traditional liturgy, helping modern men and women find new wisdom in Jewish prayer, and bring liturgy into their lives. Each book includes Hebrew text, modern translation, and commentaries from all perspectives of the Jewish world.
Vol. 1—The *Sh'ma* and Its Blessings
7 x 10, 168 pp, Hardcover, ISBN 1-879045-79-6 **$24.99**
Vol. 2—The *Amidah*
7 x 10, 240 pp, Hardcover, ISBN 1-879045-80-X **$24.95**
Vol. 3—*P'sukei D'zimrah* (Morning Psalms)
7 x 10, 240 pp, Hardcover, ISBN 1-879045-81-8 **$24.95**
Vol. 4—*Seder K'riat Hatorah* (The Torah Service)
7 x 10, 264 pp, Hardcover, ISBN 1-879045-82-6 **$23.95**
Vol. 5—*Birkhot Hashachar* (Morning Blessings)
7 x 10, 240 pp, Hardcover, ISBN 1-879045-83-4 **$24.95**
Vol. 6—*Tachanun* and Concluding Prayers
7 x 10, 240 pp, Hardcover, ISBN 1-879045-84-2 **$24.95**
Vol. 7—Shabbat at Home
7 x 10, 240 pp, Hardcover, ISBN 1-879045-85-0 **$24.95**
Vol. 8—*Kabbalat Shabbat* (Welcoming Shabbat in the Synagogue)
7 x 10, 240 pp, Hardcover, ISBN 1-58023-121-7 **$24.99**

About Jewish Lights

People of all faiths and backgrounds yearn for books that attract, engage, educate, and spiritually inspire.

Our principal goal is to stimulate thought and help all people learn about who the Jewish People are, where they come from, and what the future can be made to hold. While people of our diverse Jewish heritage are the primary audience, our books speak to people in the Christian world as well and will broaden their understanding of Judaism and the roots of their own faith.

We bring to you authors who are at the forefront of spiritual thought and experience. While each has something different to say, they all say it in a voice that you can hear.

Our books are designed to welcome you and then to engage, stimulate, and inspire. We judge our success not only by whether or not our books are beautiful and commercially successful, but by whether or not they make a difference in your life.

For your information and convenience, at the back of this book we have provided a list of other Jewish Lights books you might find interesting and useful. They cover all the categories of your life:

Bar/Bat Mitzvah
Bible Study / Midrash
Children's Books
Congregation Resources
Current Events / History
Ecology
Fiction: Mystery, Science Fiction
Grief / Healing
Holidays / Holy Days
Inspiration
Kabbalah / Mysticism / Enneagram

Life Cycle
Meditation
Parenting
Prayer
Ritual / Sacred Practice
Spirituality
Theology / Philosophy
Travel
Twelve Steps
Women's Interest

Stuart M. Matlins, Publisher

Or phone, fax, mail or e-mail to: **JEWISH LIGHTS Publishing**
Sunset Farm Offices, Route 4 • P.O. Box 237 • Woodstock, Vermont 05091
Tel: (802) 457-4000 • Fax: (802) 457-4004 • www.jewishlights.com
Credit card orders: **(800) 962-4544** (8:30AM–5:30PM ET Monday–Friday)
Generous discounts on quantity orders. SATISFACTION GUARANTEED. Prices subject to change.